THE TEXT OF REVELATION

THE TEXT OF REVELATION

A REVISED THEORY

BY

JOHN OMAN

Principal, Westminster College
Cambridge

CAMBRIDGE

AT THE UNIVERSITY PRESS

1928

CAMBRIDGE
UNIVERSITY PRESS

University Printing House, Cambridge CB2 8BS, United Kingdom

Cambridge University Press is part of the University of Cambridge.

It furthers the University's mission by disseminating knowledge in the pursuit of education, learning and research at the highest international levels of excellence.

www.cambridge.org
Information on this title: www.cambridge.org/9781107505377

First published 1928
First paperback edition 2015

A catalogue record for this publication is available from the British Library

ISBN 978-1-107-50537-7 Paperback

CONTENTS

PREFACE

MY old students, Mr Eric Philip and Mr T. W. Manson, have read this work in proof. To Mr Manson, whose knowledge of Hebrew idiom is vastly greater than mine, I owe a good many suggestions. Yet in spite of his help, there is more Hebrew idiom than my translation shows, and especially in the effect of the participle and the sequence of tenses. I am also indebted to Mr J. M. Edmonds of Jesus College, Cambridge. Not only is he very learned in all such matters generally, but he has done a similar work on Theophrastus, which gave him an especial interest as well as special knowledge. He thought the general reasoning sound, and took more trouble than I know how to acknowledge, to make the argument clearer and the translation more precise. Prof. J. M. Creed has given me some valuable criticisms from the standpoint of one who still favours the view that the condition of the text is due to conflation of sources. The note at the end is mainly an attempt to deal with them, though one or two of the criticisms are from others.

JOHN OMAN

WESTMINSTER COLLEGE
CAMBRIDGE 1928

PART I

THE TEXT & ITS REARRANGEMENT

I

SECTIONS AND GLOSSES

FOUR years ago I published a work on the Book of Revelation in which I rearranged the text on the basis of a theory that it consists of twenty-seven exactly equal sections. These were held to be 33 lines of Gebhardt's edition of the New Testament.

While attempting to arrange part of the text, on the view that the two women were parallel ideas—one representing the Divine Rule and the other the World-Rule—I noticed that I was moving a little over a page of the Gebhardt text I was using, or multiples of it, each time. When this was applied to the whole book, it wrought out with unexpected precision, except in three cases. Two passages, when put together, made exactly two sections (XXIII–XXIV); but the other, which is now § XI, was different from the rest, and the solution offered always appeared unsatisfactory.

But the working out of this theory had an obvious weakness. While the length of the sections was rigidly objective, the glosses were subjective, and it was possible to suppose that I had selected them to suit the length of the sections. Nor, as now appears when there is also an objective standard of glosses, was this suspicion without justification.

Sometime after I had turned to quite different work, and seemed to have dismissed the whole matter from my mind, it occurred to me that a great many of the passages I had treated as glosses were doublets, and that the correct test of all glosses might be that they are repetitions.

That anything so obvious should have escaped attention from the first is a mysterious, but common experience. Most people, who have concentrated attention upon work involving much detail, have found, on relaxing it, defects which it seems inconceivable that they should have overlooked.

But there was also a reason. I started with the ordinary idea of a gloss, as of the nature of a comment. Thus, in the Messages to the Churches, I said that the omission of all the repetitions of "He that hath an ear", except the last, gave a more accurate result. Yet I was so much determined by the idea of a gloss as a comment that I left the first, though it was absurd to speak of what the Spirit says to the Churches when only one Church had been mentioned, and omitted the passage about the "seven stars that are the angels of the seven churches". As I went on, it became plain that the author does thus comment on his visions, and I should have seen, therefore, that this comment should stand, and instead all the doublets go out.

The new test has discovered other errors in my previous treatment, and I have no wish to explain them away. The door opens with two keys and I had only one in hand at the time. All the same, much was done which was right.

Here, however, I wish to insist only on one point. This is that the division of the book into sections and the standard of them as exactly 33 lines of Gebhardt's text is only confirmed by this new test of glosses. This length, it will be seen, works with more rigid accuracy than before, while the sections are as they were first determined. This was done without any consideration of glosses; and they were published without any thought of the gloss as a doublet. Nor could their boundaries well be altered, because they are separated by quite decisive breaks.

In any case the divisions were made without thought of doublets, and then the removal of all free doublets—that is doublets not guaranteed by the context—makes them, with quite astonishing precision, of equal length. Surely this must be more than an accident.

A common way of criticising work of this kind is to fasten on what seems weakest, and then to dismiss the whole as equally unconvincing. One critic dismissed the previous book as the work of a twentieth-century philosopher, who could have no understanding of the mind of a first-century Christian. In any case, the criticism could only apply to the commentary, which might be all wrong, yet the re-arrangement of the text right. In the order of probability interpretation must necessarily be last: and, till the other probabilities are settled, it had perhaps better not appear at all, as in the present work.

Again attacks were made on special points, but obviously a great many points might be wrong, yet the general theory be right. Thus the broken pages might not be made up correctly or the order not be rightly determined, and yet the theory of the book as divided into equal sections be true.

An argument of this kind is not all as weak as its weakest link, but there is an order of probability in the various points, the higher probabilities not being affected by the lower. In this case, the question which is first and on which all the others depend, but which does not depend on them, is the length of the sections and the nature of the glosses.

The test of glosses now is that they are all doublets, that is to say repetitions by the original editor from his author. And what is more, so far as I have been able to detect them, the glosses include every doublet in the whole book not guaranteed by its context: and that means almost every exact doublet in the book.

With respect to the length of the sections, it may be asked why Gebhardt's text should be made the standard.

The first reason is that it happened to be the text by which this division into equal sections was first noticed: and this was the easier that the length happens to end exactly with the line. This may be accounted for by some general impression the editor had gathered from the study of MSS., or it may be a pure accident. But, if it is an accident, it is a very convenient one, as it is much easier to count exact lines than if it were always necessary to reckon with a fraction.

The lines have been approximately reproduced in the text which follows and the sections accurately: and this affords the reader a test for controlling the result, so as to be sure that the length was determined beforehand, and never depends on the present printing.

Still more important is the fact that no edition I have come across seems to be spaced so accurately. Almost any closely printed text gives the same result, but not with the same precision: and where there is difference, the comparison always seems to be in favour of Gebhardt's. Von

Soden's text, however, runs almost exactly parallel. But it is 26⅕ lines, which is less easy to calculate. The case I have discovered most different is where Von Soden has printed the number of the beast in full, where it is to that extent longer than the usual length, which confirms Gebhardt's view that the letters are the original. Tischendorf's text also works fairly accurately with 33½ lines.

The original, of course, had no spaces between the words, but the spaces seem to average out more accurately than the average of the width of letters, which in Greek was considerable, some letters being more than twice the width of others. There are two reasons why Von Soden's text and Gebhardt's are more reliable than the others. Both are printed in a type which corresponds fairly exactly to the breadth of the Greek uncial, and in a long line, which makes the adjustment at the end less frequent. They are also closely printed. Not only is this more like a closely written Greek MS., but, the wider the spacing, the less obvious any slight difference in it is; and this over a whole section might make an appreciable difference.

Supposing the MS. were written on a page somewhat like an Aramaic palimpsest in our library, which was bequeathed to us by the late Mrs Lewis, each line of which is complete and without any breaks, and written with beautiful regularity, a well printed text might be a much more accurate reproduction than any MS. of the New Testament we now possess.

The earliest we have are 250 years later than John wrote; they are large volumes written for public use; they are written in columns with short lines; and, finally, they have contractions, which are probably a later device.

But the standard is also tested by the result, as well as the result by the standard. In more than half the sections at least there is no question about the glosses, as they are all the doublets. When they are removed, the Gebhardt text is always exact, which could hardly be, unless it were an exact measure. But how this is a test of the standard of length will be more easily understood after we have seen how the tests of doublets and of length work in the simpler cases.

II

THE COMPLETE SECTIONS

WE shall assume for the present the correctness of the re-arrangement of the text which follows, and deal with the sections as there numbered.

We shall begin with the sections which seem to be whole as they stand. That is to say, nothing has been taken from them, and nothing inserted into them except doublets. We begin with them because they present the easiest problem.

These sections are I–IV, VI–X, XIII–XVI, XIX–XX. As there is no § VII—the reason for which will be given later—this means 14 sections. There are 27 in all, so this is more than half the whole book.

§§ I–IV are continuous. When all repetitions of "He that hath an ear, let him hear what the Spirit says to the churches" are omitted except one, which is naturally the last (iii. 22), the result is exactly four sections of 33 lines each.

A critic complains that this takes away from the sonorousness of the reading. This may well be, because adding to the sonorousness seems to be one reason, possibly the only one, for these and a good many other doublets.

In § VI, xi. 7 "that comes up from the abyss" is from xvii. 8 (p. 66). There it describes the devil. Here we have only to do with the beast which is the world-power.

§§ VIII–IX are continuous. The only doublet is in xiii. 9, "He that hath an ear, let him hear", which is again a doublet of iii. 22. Besides, no one is here speaking.

§§ XIII–XVI are continuous. There are exactly four lines too many for four sections. Three doublets are obvious. First, xvi. 21 "And men blasphemed God from the plague of the hail", is from *vv.* 9 and 11 above, with hail added from the previous verse. "Because" explains why the hail, which seems to be the symbol of terror, was so enormous. It was not natural, but, in a special way, supernatural.

In xviii. 15 "They stand afar off because of fear of her

torment"; and in *v.* 18 "afar off...seeing the smoke of her burning": both from *vv.* 9 and 10 above.

Each of these doublets is almost exactly a line. The rest is made up of words or short phrases: and about them there cannot be the same certainty. The repetition of "and goes into destruction" in xvii. 11 from *v.* 8 above is, however, certain. "The great city" is repeated with suspicious frequency, and "small and great" seems to be in favour with the editor. In xviii. 10 "Babylon the strong city" is not strengthened by having the great city before it. Therefore, "the city, the great" is almost certainly a gloss.

The other three or four words, it may be admitted, are selected somewhat on grounds of interpretation. The first is "the great" in xvi. 19. "Great" in the book is always supernatural, in the sense of being above nature, and it is a counterpart of the natural. Thus, if there is a great Euphrates, there is a natural Euphrates. And here the repetition of "the great city" is to keep it distinct from an ordinary city or government. This is the usual summary, and what happens is told in more detail in xvii. 12. The "three" here should be "ten" as there. The present "city" or government, which could hardly have been mentioned more particularly, will fall to pieces, each proconsul setting up for himself, and then "the great city"—which is very much what we mean by civilisation—will meet its doom. xi. 13 refers to the same event: and it is "city" alone and has "a tenth".

The other is xix. 5 "the small and great". This the author seems to keep for cases where differences of worldly state are involved, which cannot be the case here. The usage of a wider class after a narrower in this form is somewhat characteristic of the author. "Praise him all his servants, yea all fearing him."

Here we may raise the important question of whether we are excluding all doublets not required by the context, or are there many more, and we are only selecting from them?

In no other case, so far, has there been anything left even resembling a free doublet, or, beyond a word or two, a repetition at all. But here two clauses are left which have at least resemblances to other clauses.

The first is xvi. 18 "And there were lightnings and voices and thunders". This is the only one left at the end, and such atmospheric phenomena are natural when the vial is poured out on the air. While the editor might have collected them together, it is much more probable that the author had them together in one place. And, if so, this is the most likely. The chief objection is the way "And a great earthquake took place" follows it. But the difficulty arises from wrong pointing. "Lightnings, voices and thunders" end the setting, or, as it were, the paragraph. Then the narrative begins—There was a daimonic revolution to start with.

The second is xvii. 14 "Because He is lord of lords and king of kings". This seems to come in awkwardly between the "Lamb" and "those with Him": and we have the same phrase in xix. 16, the only difference being the reversal of the order of the titles. But even this change is not likely to have been made by the editor; and the difficulty is again with the pointing. There should be no comma after "kings." The Lamb conquers them because He is "lord of lords and king of kings" and *because* "those with Him are called, elect and faithful".

§ XIX is exact when the repetitions of the breaking of the second to the sixth seals are removed. Only the first and the last are mentioned, because, obviously, nothing can be read out of a roll till all its seals are broken.

§ XX vii. 5–8 is merely a mathematical doublet of the 144,000 in the previous verse. Equal numbers from tribes so unequal, the author, who knew his country, would not be likely to have made. Besides he is speaking of spiritual Israel. The other is in *v.* 2 "to whom it was given to hurt the earth and the sea", which is a prosy reproduction of the following verse with "it was given" from elsewhere.

This makes all these 14 sections exact.

In this larger half of the book all glosses are doublets of the same decorative type, either easily remembered phrases or from the immediate context. Moreover, not only are they all the free doublets: but, so far as I can discover, all the doublets. Nor is the length merely approximate, as it was when I was guessing glosses, but is, in every case, precise almost to a word.

Up to this point better proof for equal sections could scarcely be produced: and it is at least good *prima facie* evidence for applying the same idea to the rest of the book.

III

THREE CASES OF SINGLE OMISSIONS

IN dealing with these fourteen sections, it was only necessary to seek out all that could be doublets, and the length came of itself. If passages have been interpolated or removed, this is no longer possible. But if the passages are restored because they fit the context, and then, when the free doublets are removed, they fill exactly the spaces required, it should be very little less convincing.

As it is well to limit as far as possible the field of greater perplexity, we shall begin with what is simplest. These are three sections. But, as two go together, we have only to do with the restoration of two passages. One has been restored to the beginning of § V and the other to the beginning of § XVII. Should this be right, both the place and the number we shall find to be important.

The passage which has been restored to § V is xxii. 10–12.

The reasons for removing it from its present place are:

(1) There is a second "he says to me", which the author does not use elsewhere when the same speaker is continuing.

(2) To introduce the "prophecy of this book" and then to re-introduce it a little later is also unlike his work.

(3) It will be found that in order to make room for it, the editor has removed a passage, which, from its connexion with what follows, certainly belongs here.

(4) Reasons will be given afterwards for believing that, in the order in which the editor found his MSS., § V immediately followed xxii, and, therefore, if he were embarrassed by this passage, he inserted it where he could most easily dispose of it.

(5) It will be found that at the close of xxii. 17 he has an appeal about "this prophecy", which makes this passage superfluous in the place it now occupies.

The reasons for inserting it in § V are:

(1) That, if the author closed one prophecy with an appeal about its words, he would probably close another in a similar way; and the only other prophecy is the Messages to the Churches.

(2) It exactly suits this purpose. No other part of the book speaks in the same way of reward, and no ending could be found to the Messages more appropriate than, "Lo I come quickly, and my reward with me, to give to each as his work is".

The missing passage was originally rightly sought in ch. xxii, but, the existence of doublets not being then suspected and the only test being length, this passage seemed to be too long. But when the doublet (xxii. 13) which follows it and seemed to be part of it, is removed, the rest fits in with perfect exactness, not being merely approximately exact as before, but having the word over the five lines which makes it precise.

In this section there are no doublets, and the result is exactly 33 lines.

In §§ XVII–XVIII, "To Him that sitteth on the throne" in iv. 9 is a doublet of *v.* 10^{b}. There is no need to repeat to whom the praise is given: and to have it in the same form within a line or two is quite unlike the author. iv. 5 "Lightnings and voices and thunders" are a favourite decoration of the editor. Therefore, they are always suspect. That he should have introduced it here, however, entirely without suggestion from the original is improbable. But that he may have expanded what he found is another matter. Voices and thunders, where there is solemn praise and finally solemn silence, are more than suspect. Besides voices would be as elsewhere "from" the throne, not "out of" it. But lightnings are probable.

In the introduction we find a passage which suits both the length and the context. Moreover, it is followed by a passage from iv. 8, which shows that, when the editor wrote it in the introduction, he had the page we call § XVII before him. The passage is i. 7 "Lo He comes with clouds" etc. If the present connexion is right, it is a wholly suitable conclusion to the previous section. This makes §§ XVII–XVIII exact to a word. The section is a line short, the doublets are 1½ and the passage restored 2½.

The problem of understanding the editor's action here is quite simple. Not having his pages in right order, he found passages at the beginning of the pages irrelevant, and was forced to remove them to a context where the irrelevance was at least less obtrusive. Possibly one of the reasons for producing an introduction was to find a home for such stray passages, to which no other context in the book offered hospitality.

With this we shall also take § XII, because it also is simple.

As there are no doublets, the problem of its shortness was rightly solved before, on the tests of context and length. The missing passage is xix. 19[c]–20. In the context where it now stands it is impossible, because a wine-press of wrath has no relation to a blessed vintage, which is the subject there (§ XIV). The only place in the book where it does fit in is after xiv. 15. It suits this context perfectly and makes the section exact.

Yet here we have another kind of procedure, which shows a deeper perplexity. To remove a passage from the middle of a page is a different matter from merely disposing of a part at the beginning, the real connexion of which had been lost.

The reason for this we shall have to consider later, but in the sections yet to be considered, we shall find that the perplexity, and the confusion arising from it, deepen.

But this section is more than a transition to this more difficult problem. It also shows what the editor did when in doubt. He settled the content purely by verbal similarity.

We can now see how all these results are a test of the Gebhardt text as a standard of length. So long as we were using this standard for determining both the length and the glosses, it was always possible that it varied from the original, and that by ingenuity the glosses were selected to suit this variation. But in 14 sections, which is more than half the book, 12 have only short doublets, which are exact repetitions, and they are all the doublets to be found, and the doublets in the other two sections are the same as in my former book. It was only necessary to leave out all doublets, and the length came of itself with quite astonishing exactness.

To four more sections three passages have been restored. The reason for restoring them is that they suit the context, not that they fill the space; yet again the length is quite exact.

How could this happen, unless the standard were to a remarkable degree reliable? Even if we had no further check on it in the other nine sections, it would not be unreasonable to assume the trustworthiness of the standard. But there also the tests of glosses as doublets, and of transpositions by relevance or irrelevance, are independent of the length; and if the length works out exactly, the result still remains a test of the standard of length, as well as of the glosses and transpositions.

IV

§ XI

CH. viii. 6–12 AND xv. 5–xvi. 16

IN the previous work I said it was strange that the editor did not observe the injunction, not to add to the book, when he evidently took such great care not to take from it. But, from the sections already considered, the answer would seem to be that he did not think that repeating from his author was adding "to the words of the prophecy".

We also see what measure of liberty he allowed himself. He might explain the 144,000 as 12,000 from each tribe, and say 'it was given to do' what was not being done at the moment. But mostly he repeats doublets with verbal accuracy: and, so far, all he uses could quite easily be purely from memory, or from what was immediately before him.

But if the editor no more added than took from the words of his book, we cannot simply dismiss the introduction and the epilogue and the first four trumpets, as I did before. As soon as we consider them, we find that a good part of them is doublet, but by no means all. The rest of the introduction, besides what we have already dealt with, is related to ch. xxii, and we shall leave it till this comes to be considered. But the passage about the first four trumpets has very marked resemblances to the first four vials. As this latter is now before us, we shall deal with the two passages together.

The argument for holding viii. 6–12 not to be genuine is the same as before. On the theory of equal sections, it goes out on length, the section being the right length without it. Also it is inconsistent with what follows. In the first trumpet (*v.* 7) all green grass is burned; and in the fifth (ix. 4) it is all to be spared.

But it is also to a large extent doublet: in the sixth (ix. 15) we have 'a third', which is repeated in the first four in a way unlikely to be the author's. The earth, the sea, the waters, the sun are the same as in the first four vials (xvi. 2–9). "He cast it into the earth" is from viii. 5, just above or in exact form in xii. 4.

Yet it is not all doublet. The four first angels will be afterwards accounted for, but of what is ascribed to them several clauses have no originals elsewhere.

The problem, therefore, is both the resemblances and the differences between the first four trumpets and the first four vials, *i.e.* viii. 6–12 and xv. 6–xvi. 9.

Possibly the editor, not finding anything else resembling the four trumpets, at first thought the vials the same as the trumpets. Or, as he becomes more liberal with interpolations at this point, he may have thought it his duty to make up for what he deemed lost. On realising that he would be in the same difficulty with the vials, of which there were certainly seven, he seems to have replaced or spared a little, and to have borrowed from elsewhere to make up the rest.

The first problem is to discover what this borrowed material in § XI is.

The first passage (xv. 6^{b}–8) is merely a transposition forced on the editor by his identification of the angels of the vials with the angels of the last plagues. He had to put the giving of the vials to them after their last appearance. But, as these angels were, as a matter of fact, quite different, the result is to transfer a passage from another section, which, though placed just before § XI by the editor, is not connected with it. This passage, therefore, has to be restored to § XXIV.

The second passage which is unlike the rest of the section is xvi. 4^b–7. There is no angel of the altar here, and the angel of the waters is likely to have been in heaven, while this transaction is upon earth. This passage, therefore, must be restored to the only place where the angel of the altar is mentioned, which is in § XXI.

The third (xvi. 15) is evidently spoken by Jesus and is besides quite irrelevant here. Therefore, it must be restored to § XXVI, where Jesus is speaking, and where, as we shall find, what follows guarantees the connexion.

We shall now consider the doublets in both passages.

In viii. 7–10, it is easier to say what is not doublet. *v.* 7 "And there was hail and fire mingled with blood"; "And the third of the trees and all green grass was burned"; *v.* 8 "As a great mountain burning with fire"; *v.* 10 "And there fell from the sky a great star blazing like a torch"; the whole of *v.* 11. The rest is all doublet, mainly from ch. xvi with suggestions from *vv.* 5 and 6 above, and, for *v.* 12, from ix. 2 and vi. 12.

In xv. 5–xvi. 21 the most certain doublet is xvi. 2 "having the mark of the beast, and worshipping his image" from xiii. 15 and 17. In *v.* 9 "Of Him who has power" has more than one source, and "to blaspheme the name of God for the plagues" is a more probable reading.

There are further two words doubtful: in *v.* 3 "blood" from *v.* 4; and in *v.* 12 "Great" from ix. 14. There Euphrates seems to be the supernatural stream, Oceanus; here it seems to be the ordinary Euphrates, dried up for the passing of human armies.

The text is the best I can do to put what remains of both passages together, and restore from viii. what has been taken from xvi. That this is all correct is far from being affirmed, but nothing original has been left out, and the result is, as nearly as anything so complicated can be calculated, the exact length.

The 'thirds' are most doubtful. They may all have been imported from ix. 15 and beyond question the editor multiplies them as a distinction from the vials. But, as the vials are ordinary historical happenings, the author may have spoken of thirds in one or two places.

V

SECTIONS WITH OMISSIONS

§§ XXI–XXIV

§§ XXI–XXII (viii. 1–ix. 21) are continuous.

We have removed viii. 7–12 and restored, after viii. 5, xvi. 4^b–6^b. xvi. 6^c "for they are worthy" is a doublet of iii. 5. As it is there said of the saints, it is not likely to have been applied also by the author to the wicked.

viii. 5^c is a doublet of xvi. 18. In another case also this display is put in where something has been removed. As the passage stands, nothing else happens—a feeble ending for so dramatic a setting. The restoration gives a dramatic climax.

In *v.* 13^c "trumpet" is singular, which suggests that the rest has been added. If we also omit "the remaining" and "three", it reads "For the blasts of the trumpet", which is just trumpet-blasts. Moreover, that this proclamation is at the beginning, and not in the middle, is more likely in itself and much more like the method of the author.

In ix. 2 "from the smoke of the pit" is a quite needless repetition of what is already in the same verse.

In *v.* 4 "the grass of the earth nor aught green nor any tree" is a doublet from viii. 7, and makes an impossible reading here. "Except those not having God's seal" must be opposed to those who have it, and not to grass and trees.

v. 18 is a doublet of *vv.* 15 and 17. In the first place, these woes are not elsewhere called plagues; in the second, they have not yet all taken place; in the third, only in this one is there fire and brimstone from mouths and a third of men killed.

v. 19 "in the mouth of the horses" at first sight seems doubtful, especially as mouth is singular and tails plural. But it can be read: for, though their power is thus in the mouth, their real power is in their tails. This seems to be a vision of sin, the idea coming from Prov. xxxii. 23

"At last it biteth like a serpent", and perhaps from the whole idea of the wages of sin.

This leaves us with something slightly short of the length.

But ix. 14 is impossible as it stands. Why should "the sixth angel" be repeated at all? He has just been mentioned, and no mention of any other angel has intervened. "To him" would have been enough. Still more, why should he be described as having the trumpet when he has just blown it? Again, angels in the rest of the book are always ambassadors of God, not destroying forces. Finally, it is not four angels, but myriads of hosts that are let loose; and they have not in the least the aspect of angels.

In vii. 1 we have four angels standing at the four corners of the earth, holding back the forces of destruction. In Zech. vi. 5 we find that the spirits at the corners of the earth "come forth from standing before the Lord". Last time I argued that these are the first four of the 'angels who stand before the Lord' to whom the trumpets were given. This was a right conclusion, but at that time I did not know enough about the editor's ways of dealing with the text to see how they came in in ix. 14.

From his having made the first four already blow trumpets and from his ignorance of the Old Testament origin of their nature, the editor was naturally perplexed by finding four more provided with trumpets. He settled the matter by doing as little violence to the words as possible. As he had already made the angels blow, he omits their blowing here the more readily. Elsewhere also he omits in its right place what he has already entered in a doublet. Then the rest was only a question of re-arrangement and change of case and number.

Probably there is not a second reference to the corners of the earth, because the four corners of the golden altar is the heavenly counterpart, and the voice from them may have been thought by the author to be sufficient reference. "The great Euphrates" is Oceanus—the stream which goes round the earth, with the corners outside of it. The forces to be let loose are in the corners of the earth outside of it, and prevented by the four angels from crossing it.

The command now comes to set them free: and this is done by blowing their trumpets.

The reading adopted makes least change in the text, but it may be the angels which are 'on the great river Euphrates', which might be a synonym for the four corners of the earth, and the command be simply, "Loose those bound", meaning those you are restraining. Also "the others" in viii. 13 may be from this. But as this is doubtful, we read, "saying to the four angels—those having trumpets, 'Loose those restrained on the river, the Great Euphrates.' Then the four angels blew: and there were set free those prepared".

This explains what the four angels in vii. 1 are waiting for and does not leave them at their task of restraining for ever; it explains why the first four trumpets are not blown earlier; it keeps angels to their usual tasks; it does not confuse four angels with myriads of hosts.

§§ XXIII–XXIV also go together.

§ XXIII is the only one which, in the strict sense, has been divided. The first part is xi. 14–19, while the rest does not follow till xiv. 6.

Like all the other sections, these sections were in my former book as they are now. The original reasons for putting these passages together were, first, the connexion, and, second, that they made up the length of two sections.

The connexion is as before, and is reasonably clear, but the argument from the length depended on the fact that the doublets added and a passage transferred elsewhere are almost the same length. Yet now this argument is still stronger, because the slight difference makes the sections exact and not, as before, a word or two short.

Two doublets are so very literal and irrelevant that I was extremely dull not to have detected them before.

(1) xiv. 8 "Another angel, a second, followed after, saying 'Fallen, fallen is Babylon the Great, etc.'".

This is (*a*) extremely irrelevant. Babylon is nowhere on the horizon; (*b*) as another angel goes before, this is not the second, but the third; (*c*) a third does follow correctly, if this is removed, and what he says also follows what goes before; (*d*) it is literally from xviii. 1–3. There it is in place, and "another angel, a second" really is the second.

The other is xiv. 11 "And the smoke of their torment goes up for ever and ever, and they have no rest day and night, those worshipping the beast and his image, and, if anyone receives the mark of his name." This is all doublet.

The latter half is an exact repetition from *v*. 9, just above, which repetition of himself is not characteristic of the author. "They have no rest day and night" is from iv. 8, where the reference is to ceaseless praise, and, therefore, is not likely to have been used by the author for ceaseless torment. "Their smoke goes up for ever and ever" is from xix. 3. "Their torment" follows the previous verse "they are tormented". There it is not eternal torment, but the torment of the final woe upon earth, which is not eternal.

Nowhere in what I take to be the author's own text is there eternal torment. On the contrary, the lake of fire is the destruction of all that cannot belong to the final perfect state, and death and Hades end in it as well as the wicked.

In xi. 19 we have the largest display of physical phenomena in the book—lightnings, voices, thunders, earthquake, great hail. This is the third doublet of this kind and all point to xvi. 18 as the original. The first was "lightnings, voices and thunders", as in 18[a]; the second added earthquake from the next clause; this adds great hail from *v*. 21. Also in xi. 18 "to small and great" is a doublet, and irrelevant.

This is the section to which xv. 6[b]–xvi. 1 has been restored (p. 88). It follows xv. 1 and is a description of the angels of the Last Plagues and their work. As in Isaiah's vision (Is. vi. 4) the temple fills with smoke. Even the redeemed cannot enter, but they appear beside the heavenly sea, which still separates them from it.

But before this final destruction, there has been an ingathering of all the good. From this xiv. 19[b]–20 has been removed, as inappropriate to a blessed vintage, and restored to § XII.

The whole, as it stands, is 68 lines.

The passage put in is 8, that taken out 3. The doublets are 1, $2\frac{1}{2}$, $3\frac{1}{2} = 7$. This leaves 66, or two exact sections.

The only other possible doublet is xv. 6[b]. "Girt about

the breasts with a golden girdle," which is like i. 13. But it is not exact, and the symbol might resemble Christ's, to show that their work was not destruction, but preparation for his rule, which immediately follows.

VI

THE INTRODUCTION AND xix. 9–10

BEFORE entering on the last four sections, we shall consider the introduction, because, most of the doublets in it being from this part, it was evidently before the editor at the time, and some of what is not doublet may also be from it.

"Apocalypse" is not found elsewhere, either as a substantive or a verb. As the work was expected to go along with other Christian books, a title may have been imperative; and, as the editor is evidently speaking in his own name, he may have allowed himself this latitude. The rest of *vv.* 1 and 2 is from xxii. 6–8 and i. 9.

But *v.* 3 is not a doublet, and we shall see that it goes with what follows. Most of what follows also has no original, and therefore, on our test, is itself original.

vv. 4–6 are the most perplexing.

"John to the seven churches which are in Asia" is not likely because the whole book is for all God's servants, and xxii. 21 has "upon all". Therefore this is probably a doublet of i. 11, with "In Asia", to save repetition of the names. This resembles Paul's usual form of signing his letters at the beginning, which may be the source of the suggestion. But this book as a whole is not a letter: nor is this John's way of introducing himself.

A blessing and a doxology might somewhere be a suitable ending: and this is the more probably original that "peace" does not occur elsewhere except in vi. 4. But "to take away peace from the earth" is certainly not a parallel. Rather we should expect that somewhere in the book peace be restored to the saints.

v. 8 is plainly a doublet from xxi. 6 and iv. 8 with a slight change in the order of the clauses. In *v.* 4 "from He who is" is the more certainly from the same source, that the lack of grammatical connexion between the preposition and object shows it to be a quotation. "The seven spirits which are before the throne" is from iv. 5. This is confirmed by the repetitions of "from" which is unlike the author's rapid style.

The "seven spirits who are before the throne" as the middle term of a trinity with God and Christ, seems to have no accord with the author's way of regarding them. Even for the editor it is singular, but the probable explanation is that he identified them with the angels of the churches, and, as he is here thinking specially of these churches, he thought a salutation from them to the churches appropriate. But that the author identified them is unlikely.

Having introduced them, the editor could not leave God out. But in the original this special description of the Almighty has to do with his rule over the past, the present and the future, which is there being considered, and it is not used, as here, as a general name of God.

"To Him be the glory and the power for ever and ever. Amen." might be from v. 13. But it omits "praise and honour", which is not the editor's way, and it is not a free doublet, being necessary to complete i. 6.

In xxii. 21 we have a blessing from Jesus Christ alone, and in this passage he alone is prominent.

Therefore, the probable reading of i. 4–6 is "Grace and peace from Jesus Christ" to the end.

One other doublet has a bearing on the last sections, and we shall consider it also before going on to deal with them. This is xix. 9–10.

It is clearly a doublet of xxii. 9–10. That the latter is in the original context is also clear. But the connexion only becomes plain when we put the two passages together. "The witness of Jesus is the spirit of prophecy" in xix. 10 would have no meaning if the prophets had not been mentioned. But they are only mentioned in xxii. 9.

Here we have an example of the editor's method, which he employs again in at least one case of very great importance. He does not copy the whole of the original in the doublet, and he does not always repeat in the original place all he has already written in the doublet.

For our present purpose this is the special lesson of xix. 9–10, but we shall afterwards find that the place it occupies is also evidence for the order of the pages as the editor found them.

VII

THE LAST FOUR SECTIONS

THE part of the book covered by the last four sections is from the beginning of ch. xx. to the end. This divides plainly into four parts: (1) ch. xx. 1–10; (2) xx. 11–xxi. 8; (3) xxi. 9–xxii. 17; (4) the epilogue xxii. 18–21.

In my former arrangement, I held that the second (xx. 11–xxi. 8) was the close, and was by itself. Of this, we shall find confirmation.

The first and third were regarded as making up between them the other three sections, while the epilogue was regarded as an addition by the editor. Both conclusions we shall find to be mistaken; but the reason for the mistake was that the editor puts in doublets of very much the same length as the passages he inserts elsewhere, the discovery of which was impossible without this test of glosses as doublets.

We are not, however, concerned with former mistakes on inadequate tests: and we must start afresh on the whole passage, only keeping in mind these natural divisions in it.

(*a*) § XXVII

We shall deal with the text as arranged by the editor, and begin with ch. xx. 1–10, which is in § XXVII.

There are two doublets. The first is *v.* 5 "This is the first resurrection", which is from the next clause. The second is in *v.* 10 "And they shall be tormented day and night for ever and ever". This is a repetition of the doublet xiv. 11, the origin of which has already been explained.

What is left is exactly 25½ lines. This leaves 7½ to make up the length of the section. This is the exact length of what was left as genuine in i. 3–6, though there was no idea of where it should go when its length was determined. The editor evidently thought that xx. 1–10 must go before, not after the description of the Holy City. Read after it, however, we have a fitting close in these verses from the introduction, following xxii. 17: and we have the usual explanation of their removal—that the page being read out of its order, the first part of it seemed to be irrelevant.

(*b*) § XXVIII

The second passage is xx. 11–xxi. 8, which is now in § XXVIII. The first doublet is xxi. 2 "and the holy city Jerusalem, the new, I saw descending out of heaven from God, prepared as a bride adorned for her husband". The first clause is the same as xxi. 10, except for "new", which is taken from the new heavens and the new earth in *v.* 1 or from ii. 12, where it is plainly just another name for the Holy Jerusalem. But it is in xxi. 9 that the holy Jerusalem is described as "the bride, the Lamb's wife", and therefore, it is there that "a bride adorned for her husband" is in place.

This is plainly a similar case to xix. 10 and xxii. 9. That is to say, a part of the passage, already written as a gloss, is not repeated in its proper place. Therefore, "a bride adorned for her husband" should be replaced in *v.* 10; and the rest of *v.* 2 goes out as a doublet which is a gloss.

This is a conclusion of the utmost importance for the order of the text. It disposes of what many have felt to be perhaps the greatest perplexity in the whole book. Several solutions have been offered, of which my own was possibly the most elaborate. Unfortunately for all this ingenuity, there is no longer any problem to solve, because the second Holy Jerusalem is a mere doublet.

xx. 14. "The lake of fire" is from the same verse.

Ch. xxi. 4 "And He shall wipe away every tear from their eyes" is from vii. 17. There it is in place after the long sorrow of the World-rule. Here it is not in place after 1000 years of the Christ-rule.

v. 5 "And he says to me, Write, that these are the faithful and true words" seems to be from the doublet in xix. 9, for "write" is taken from its context.

v. 6 "And he says to me, It is done," is from xvi. 17 where it means "It is done already".

On the other hand *v.* 6 "And I will give to him that thirsts of the fountain of the water of life freely" is not a doublet, but has an important distinction. Even in the Holy City there is only the stream. In the final, perfect state, men drink from the fountain-head.

With this we should also take xxii. 17[c]. There it is clearly an intrusion of the most obvious kind. The subject there is the coming of Jesus, and the voices that pray for his coming. But the coming in "let him come" is of a quite different kind; and there is nothing in the context to suggest the water of life. The insertion of the clause in xxii. 17 is simply the most conspicuous of many instances of making connexions by mere words. One "freely" and one "water of life" are doublets, which helps to mark the connexion. Thus xxi. 6 reads "I will give to him that thirsts of the fountain of the water of life, and he who thirsts let him come; he who wills, let him take freely".

If, as we suppose, this is the closing section, xxii. 18–19 and 21 naturally goes with it. But in it "Of those written in this book" is from *v.* 18. Where it stands it is the purest tag, connected neither by grammar nor by sense.

The first passage is 27 lines; this is 6, which is exactly 33 lines.

Though this latter part was at the end of the page, and not, as the others, at the beginning, the reason for transferring it would be much the same. Obviously it could only be at the close of the whole book. But the editor had decided that the Last Judgment must be before the Holy Jerusalem. Therefore, he could not do other than transfer it.

This is important confirmation of the view that the Last Judgment and the New Heavens and the New Earth were the final state, and that the whole section is at the end.

But the fact that the last page too was complete may also explain why, as I have tried to show, the author does not repeat himself, and why he seems, on several occasions, to have controlled the length of his writing by the page. The reason would seem to be either that his sheets were all the writing material he had, or that he had resolved on this number of sheets as the length of his book.

(*c*) §§ XXV–XXVI

In all the other sections, as soon as passages were restored to their own contexts and free doublets removed, everything fitted together at once, like the parts of a puzzle, with an exactness which seemed to afford reliable evidence of a right result. Nor was the task difficult. With a fair knowledge of the text, the only possible context was always apparent; and, when memory was not sufficient for the doublets, Bruder's Greek Concordance of the New Testament provided all information. But xxi. 9–xxii. 17 and 20, which makes §§ XXV–XXVI, did not work out in this simple way.

Two passages have already been taken away.

(1) xxii. 10–12 was transferred to § V. For restoring it, reasons were given (p. 8). But its irrelevance here is also evident. We find it introduced by "He says to me", which is not necessary as we have the same phrase just above, and, if the passage were in its right place, it would be by the same speaker. There is nothing about reward in this place, whereas it is very much to the point in the connexion to which it has been restored. Finally we should not expect "this book" to be introduced till the close of the prophecy, and even then we should expect it to be by the author, not the angel. Where it has been put it is the close of a prophecy, and by the author.

(2) xxii. 17[c] was transferred to § XXVIII. For this restoration reasons were given (p. 22). But an additional reason is the way in which its removal makes plain the meaning of what remains. Then we read "The spirit and the bride say, come; and let him who hears say, come; and he who witnesses these things says, Yea, Amen. Come Lord Jesus".

Three passages have been restored to this part, and the reasons have been given.

(1) "Coming down as a bride adorned for her husband," from xxi. 2, follows xxi. 10 (p. 21).

(2) From xix. 10 has to be restored to xxii. 9 "of those holding the witness of Jesus", and, "For the witness of

Jesus is the spirit of prophecy". How this is put together can be seen in the text, where it is plain that all the passages are necessary to each other (p. 92).

(3) "Lo I come as a thief. Blessed is he watching and keeping his garments, that he walk not naked and they see his shame" from xvi. 15. This precedes xxii. 14, because this verse is continuous with it. "Blessed is he who keeps his garments clean, yea, blessed are they who have washed their robes." As the passage inserted before it had made it superfluous in its own place, we can see why it was removed to another.

Some doublets are plain repetitions.

(1) "Except those written in the Lamb's book of life," xxi. 27, is from xiii. 8. Elsewhere they are only the 144,000. If only they enter, the exclusion of anything so gross as abomination and lie would not need to be mentioned. Moreover, the Holy City is still an earthly state, and the nations walk in the light of it. Therefore, it is not confined to the saints, and much less to the 144,000.

(2) In xxii. 5 "and night is not any more" is from xxi. 25; and that there is some kind of exchange between xxi. 23 and xxii. 5 appears from the Lamb being the lamp in xxi. 23 and the phrase which gives it meaning being in xxii. 5. This again seems to be a case of a clause being entered earlier and not repeated in its proper place. This would mean the restoration of "The Lamb is their lamp" to xxii. 5.

(3) xxii. 7 "And lo I come quickly" is from *v.* 12. In *v.* 7 we have "Blessed is he holding the words of the prophecy of this book"; in *v.* 9 "of those holding the words of this book"; in *v.* 10 "the words of the prophecy of this book". Such repetition is unlike the author. Moreover, the angel is not likely to speak of a book at all, and much less of one not yet written; the author's brethren could not be described as keeping what they could not have read; any reference to this book is likely to be by the author, and, by him, only at the end. Where *vv.* 10–12 have been restored, it is the end of the Messages to the Churches, and is by the author. There it is entirely appropriate.

"Blessed" and "keeping" in *v.* 7 are from i. 3. Where it has been restored, it also is at the end of a prophecy and by the author. There it is appropriate both in position and meaning and is sufficiently different from xxii. 9 to show that it is original.

The passages in *vv.* 7 and 9 are therefore doublets of these passages, and that they are glosses further appears from their irrelevance where they are.

(4) xxii. 13 "I am the alpha etc." is an exact doublet of xxi. 6, where it is God who speaks. In *v.* 20 "I come quickly" is as before from *v.* 12.

There are also two short doublets which are fairly certain. In xxii. 3 "the throne of God and of the Lamb" is followed by the singular pronoun. Moreover, the description of God in ch. iv. is merely "one seated on the throne." Therefore, it must be the Lamb's face and not God's that is seen. In that case we should read the "throne of the Lamb is in it". But in xxii. 1 we should probably read only "the throne of God". This is the stream of righteousness, and "the throne of God" is, throughout the book, the fountain-head of all righteousness.

In xxii. 5 "And they shall reign for ever and ever" might be from xi. 15 with only a change of number, especially as it seems to be irrelevant.

These are all transpositions and doublets of the usual type. But there are other passages which are more uncertain.

In both xxi. 24 and 26 we have "bringing glory into it". The first seems also interruption, as the subject is the light. But the question is how to deal with it.

After the numerical pattern of doublets we have had before, xxi. 13, "on the north three gates etc."; and the ordinals in 19–20 might be doublets.

There seemed no way of deciding, until it occurred to me to consider the Old Testament sources. Almost every part of the original has such a source, mostly from Isaiah, Ezekiel and Daniel.

xxi. 13 is guaranteed by Ezekiel xlii. 16–17 and xlviii. 31–34. In the first passage we have the peculiar order of the quarters—east, north, south, west, and in the latter the names of the gates after the tribes, and three facing each quarter.

In xxi. 19–20 the names of the stones are those on the high-priest's breastplate in Ex. xxviii. 17–20. Whether they are exact or not, this is unquestionably what they are meant to be, and it explains the symbolism. But the names in Rev. are not even vaguely in the order in Exodus. Moreover, "adorned with every precious stone" cannot mean that each foundation is composed wholly of one. Nor is this repetition of numbers characteristic of the author as it is of the editor. Thus we read "The foundations of the wall of the city were adorned with every precious stone—jasper, sapphire etc.".

The original of xxi. 24 is Is. lx. 3 "and nations shall come to thy light and kings to the brightness of thy rising". Probably, therefore, we should read only "and the kings of the earth", which would be a construction like "and the Lamb" in *v.* 22, the authenticity of which is guaranteed by the next verse, where the Lamb is the "lamp". Thus we read "The nations and the kings of the earth walk by the light of it".

This, so far as anything so complicated can be calculated, works out exactly as two sections, each of 33 lines.

The whole is 75¾. The two passages removed elsewhere = 6 lines. The three passages restored = about 4½. This leaves 8¼, and the doublets are as nearly as possible that length.

This is the close: and it includes every word in the book, either as text or doublet, except "The Apocalypse of Jesus Christ", which, and not "The Apocalypse of John", is its proper title.

The work has been more like the solving of a Chinese puzzle than orthodox higher criticism. This objective test of glosses, indeed, rather casts doubt on what can be determined by mere insight.

Moreover, so far as I can discover with the help of Bruder, no free doublets of any length are left. And even of short phrases the only two plainly repeated are "for ever and ever" and "small and great".

The nearest to a doublet left are i. 6 and v. 18, but this is not exact repetition, and, as both are doxologies, "for ever and ever" could not be omitted from either. The phrase is left also in vii. 12, x. 6, xi. 15, xv. 7, xix. 3 and xxii. 5. In each case it seems guaranteed both by the context and by the fact that the evanescent and the eternal are being contrasted. I have omitted it in iv. 9, xiv. 11, and xx. 10 and there both guarantees are absent.

The other phrase is "small and great". The omissions have been made on the standard of length, but the result is interesting. xi. 18 goes out, xiii. 16 stands, xix. 5 goes out, xix. 18 stands, xx. 12 stands. In all cases where it stands, it embraces all mankind; in the cases where it goes out it refers to the saints. This must be right as "small and great" is a worldly distinction.

That there should be some repetition of both phrases could hardly be avoided, seeing that the theme is so largely the eternal in contrast to the fleeting and the true greatness in contrast to earthly distinctions. But even of them the genuine repetitions are few and to the purpose: and of other repetitions I can only think of "After these things I saw", used for introducing a new phase of the subject.

Could fuller proof be given for the main thesis that the confusion of the present text is due to the transposition of pages of equal length? The value of the rest can only be determined by the measure of better sequence and clearer meaning it introduces. But this conclusion stands by itself, and, while a good use of it would be a confirmation, no inadequacy in applying it disproves it.

VIII

THE ORDER OF THE SECTIONS

IF the sections have been correctly made up, their order is reasonably evident: and that it should be so is some confirmation of at least a large measure of correctness.

There are only two changes in my former order. The first is comparatively unimportant. It is the return of what was § XII in the previous book to its place as it stands in the editor's arrangement. Perhaps the reasons for removing it were never very adequate, but with the re-arrangement which follows they entirely disappear. With this exception §§ I–XVI remain in the same order. As there is no § VII, this means 15 sections. Thus with the exception of § XII, the order of more than half the book is unchanged.

The second, however, is a radical change, giving a different character to all the latter part. What was §§ XVII–XIX now goes after what was §§ XX–XXVI. That is to say, the scene in Heaven and what follows it goes before, and not after, the account of the Holy Jerusalem. Except for this change, the rest is also in the old order.

For the arrangement of §§ I–XVI the reasons are the same as before, with the additional reason that the restoration to § V shows much more clearly its connexion with § IV.

The little roll in ch. x. is, in accordance with O. T. precedent, the beginning of the new prophecy, the Messages being the first. This is confirmed by finding it preceded by the conclusion of the Messages.

The two women represent, not actual kingdoms, but the God-rule and the World-rule. As has been said, the changes in the order of the text necessary to achieve the order which followed from this view, were the original source of the idea that the book consists of equal sections: and that this is right is plainer than before.

Babylon, the second woman, it was held, was not any earthly kingdom, such as Rome, but the World-rule, as opposed to the God-rule. This the earthly kingdoms, symbolised as beasts, merely incarnated. Judgment on these earthly kingdoms, I argued, came first; and then followed judgment upon the World-rule itself. This the new test confirms in two ways.

(*a*) On a purely objective standard of glosses, and with a greater precision of length, the divisions of the book made on the idea of this order have been justified.

(*b*) What has been restored to § XI shows much more fully that we have to do with judgments upon the World-kingdoms which have oppressed Israel, some past and some yet to come. There are the plagues of Egypt, the burning mountain of Edom, and the falling star of Babylon; and the original of the fourth vial seems to be Isaiah's prophecy against Assyria x. 16 "and under his glory shall be kindled a burning like the burning of fire", possibly combined with the sun-worship of Persia.

For the order in which I previously arranged the rest of the book, the reasons were: (*a*) that what were then § XIX and § XX (now § XXVI and § XVII) seemed to dovetail into one another, as the former was a line too long and the latter a line too short.

(*b*) That a new kind of Holy Jerusalem seemed to require some preparation to be made for it, and some kind of removal of the first.

But on the new test the extra line turns out to be a doublet which is a gloss; and the other section, as now restored, is exact and not a line too short. Now all sections are exact.

Again, on the new test of doublets as glosses, the descent of another Holy Jerusalem is found to have no existence. There is simply one Holy Jerusalem. Only, after a thousand years of rule in the present earthly state, all evil is destroyed, and its eternal order is fully consummated.

The chief argument for the new arrangement is the negative one, that there is no place for the woes after the coming of the Holy Jerusalem because there is no second Holy Jerusalem. They are the Messianic Woes, which precede the coming of the Messianic reign. That they were widely expected, the Gospels alone furnish sufficient evidence.

But this is further confirmed by the connexion with what goes before, when rightly interpreted. The close of

§ XVI is just the usual summary of the next part of the story, the narrative of which begins with § XVII and ends with the coming of the Holy Jerusalem.

The summaries are very important helps for understanding the order of the book.

The vision of one like unto a Son of Man, the living one, who has the keys of death and of Hades, in the midst of the Churches in ch. i. sums up the Messages to the Churches. Ch. xi. 1–13 (§ VI) sums up the whole story of prophecy to the end of the world-kingdoms. Ch. xvi. 17–21 (§ XIII), in the same way, sums up events to the second coming. These summaries are not part of the narrative, but the narrative which follows relates in detail the period of which the summary has given only the general character. The summaries are, therefore, as it were, introductory abstracts to the main divisions of the book.

So, in xix. 1–9 (§ XVI), we have the elders and the living creatures and the heavenly hosts and the blessed consummation: and only, thereafter, does the narrative of how this was realised begin. Thus, either to expect that the mention of the heavenly host presupposes their introduction already, or that the invitation to the marriage of the Lamb is to be followed by the coming of the Bride immediately, is a misunderstanding of the author's method.

The view on which the former arrangement was made, that the coming of the Holy Jerusalem, the Bride, must follow immediately the invitation to the marriage, was, therefore, merely such a misunderstanding. The passage is a summary, and the whole story of the preparation must precede the consummation.

Up to this point we have to do with mere human history, the completion of what had already been announced by the prophets. We are told that the little roll is a prophecy of the same kind as theirs.

But the heavenly roll is a new kind of prophecy: and, from this point, we have a judgment on the daimonic powers, from which human evil has sprung, as well as on men.

As the World-order began with war in heaven, we now return to heaven. As part of the first scene in heaven may be missing, we cannot understand fully the parallel, but there is sufficient left to show that it exists. This, in itself, is a confirmation of the arrangement now adopted.

In any case, the scene in ch. xii. could not possibly follow the scene in ch. iv.

(*a*) If the heavenly roll with seven seals had been opened, why should the seer have to prophesy afterwards from a little roll presented to him on earth by an angel?

(*b*) If the judgment which follows the opening of the heavenly roll had taken place, no milder judgments, as they appear in the editor's order, would be necessary, or even possible.

(*c*) The origin of the World-order, which we have in ch. xii, cannot possibly follow the preparation for replacing it by the Divine-order, with which the heavenly roll and what follows its opening is plainly concerned.

(*d*) If the right passage has been restored before ch. iv, as in § XVII, we have a plain connexion with xix. 9 which closes § XVI. The invitation to the marriage-supper of the Lamb is naturally followed by the announcement of his coming. Besides, the whole summary is followed by the seer being called up to heaven to learn how it is to be carried out.

§§ XVII–XX follow in the editor's order.

§ XXI also follows in the editor's order, and, apart from this, we have the opening of the book, which must follow at this point. Then, as the text has been restored, the woes follow in order. They are §§ XXII–XXIV.

The first and the clearest connexion of § XXIV with § XXV is the angels of the last plagues who have finished the whole work of God's wrath on the earth. As one of the angels of the first plagues, which destroyed the earthly kingdoms, led the seer into the wilderness to see the great harlot—the World-rule, so now one of the angels of the last plagues, which have destroyed the whole dominion of evil in the earth, leads him to a high mountain to see the coming of the other rule—the Bride of Christ, the God-rule.

The idea I had before that "last" was simply added from elsewhere was justified by the method of the editor. Yet it is perhaps the most arbitrary suggestion into which I was driven by the mistaken order of the sections, because it is extremely improbable that the same set of angels would fulfil two similar functions, more particularly as, though similar in form, they have objects so entirely different.

In the present order, that it is one of the angels of the last plagues is the plainest key to the sequence, because, having finished their work of destruction, they at once proceed to show the high end for which the destruction has taken place.

This sufficiently establishes the connexion by itself, but it is confirmed by the passage at the end of § XXIV ch. xv. 2–4, which is again the usual rapid summary of what follows.

That ch. xx–xxi. 8 is the end hardly needs discussion. The expectation, which was the hope our author set before his readers, was the Holy Jerusalem. But he held the ordinary Jewish expectation of a temporal Messianic kingdom, and probably he held it because he thought a Christ-rule just and necessary for man, after the World-rule, before final judgment. Yet, as this was a thousand years away, he summarises it rapidly. The forces of evil are let loose for a season in order to be consumed. Then all evil things as well as all evil persons are destroyed, and the Holy City continues in a new heaven and a new earth, with all sea of separation from God entirely done away, and man drinking from the fountain of life and not merely the stream.

Two passages, which refer to the same event, confirm this order. In x. 7 in the days of the seventh angel the allotted time shall be ended; in xi. 18, when the seventh angel has blown his trumpet, the time has come for the dead to be judged, to reward God's servants, and to destroy those who destroy the earth.

This might mean that the Final Judgment is to take place at once and the Final State to come. But we have still the Millennial Reign, which could not be after this. Besides, those who destroy the earth must still be on it. Therefore, we must distinguish. So far as the departed saints are concerned, their reward comes with the Holy Jerusalem. Yet, for most of them, this follows, not in the Holy City, but by the heavenly sea. At the same time the evil forces on the earth are destroyed. A judgment after a thousand years cannot be meant, but as an immediate accompaniment of Christ's rule, it might not be inconsistent with a Final Judgment later, as the time which is to end is the temporal rule up to the end of the present world-era.

This confirms the order in two ways. x. 7 assumes that all the events up to this end of time are still to be related: and xi. 18 that this point has been reached.

The only alternative is to regard the Millennial Reign and a further judgment as a later appendage. This is not improbable, especially seeing how the account of the Holy City now ends. But this would only the more certainly show these two sections to be the last.

IX

THE ORIGINAL MS. AND THE EDITOR'S ORDER

A hypothesis is here offered of the cause of the editor's perplexity which led him to make the present arrangement of the book. But this is a still further question of probability, upon which the matters already discussed do not depend. They might all be true, though we were utterly incapable of explaining how they came to pass. Reasons for the conduct, even of our personal acquaintances, are often doubtful guess-work, and the reasons for the action of a person, probably of a different mentality from ourselves and working under different conditions, might be quite beyond our guessing.

Yet it remains a problem how anyone, having any presuppositions—who, even if he were not very enlightened, was, as appears from his work, painfully conscientious, and who was also extremely anxious to arrive at the right order—should have landed in such confusion. Plainly, therefore, any suggestion which showed how this was psychologically possible, would add to the probability of the new arrangement.

The hypothesis offered may be divided into four parts, though the chief evidence is that these parts fit together. It is that (*a*) there was a missing page; (*b*) the original MS.

consisted of seven double sheets; (*c*) there were two, possibly three, broken quires; and (*d*) the editor found the quires and the broken pages in an order which was not the original order.

(*a*) *A Missing Page*

The first part of the hypothesis is that one page is missing, the page, which, on the supposition of the order here set forth, is after § VI. In the present enumeration, it will be observed, there is no § VII.

For this view there are three reasons.

1. As now arranged, the sequence elsewhere is fairly evident. But here there is a gulf with nothing to bridge it. Something surely must have gone before to explain it, of which no trace can be found anywhere in the book.

2. If the arrangement suggested be correct, the editor was aware of its absence, as he interpolates part of another page (ch. xi. 14–19) at this point, apparently thinking, at first at least, that it was the right page. The passage is irrelevant to the context, but its insertion can be explained on this hypothesis.

3. The addition of a page at this point would make up a book of seven quires of double sheets or four pages. This from the prominence of the number seven in the book is probable in itself, but the main reason is that the conception of such a book goes a long way towards explaining the order which now exists.

(*b*) *A Book of Seven Quires*

The second part of the hypothesis is that the original MS. consisted of seven quires of double sheets or four pages. To show how this would work, I have numbered the sections on the supposition of this missing page, omitting § VII. Thus reckoned we have all the pages of qq. 1. 4. 5. together in the right order. In q. 7 also, they are together, though not in the right order.

This is the more striking that the quires themselves are all separated.

Also, if we take out the part supposed above to be substituted for a lost page c of quire 2, we have what remains of it in order; and, in addition, pp. a and b of qq. 3 and 6 are together and in their right sequence.

If our order is right, however, qq. 2–4 and 5–6 have had their order reversed. But, when these are exchanged, all the sections are in order, in spite of having interpolated passages between. Moreover, it is another confirmation that the three passages which, as maintained above, were at the beginning of sections, and were removed because, owing to the disarrangement, the connexion of them could not be understood, are all at the beginning of quires (pp. 8 and 9).

(*c*) *Broken Quires*

The large interpolations consist of four sections, which in our order are §§ XI, XII, XXIII, XXIV. That is to say they are pp. c and d of quires 3 and 6. This would seem to indicate that both sheets of qq. 3 and 6 as well as the inside sheet of q. 2 were broken.

The main reason for this view is that it would explain the larger part of the confusion in the mind of the editor. But two other facts prove his difficulty with them.

First, apart from the passages at the beginning of quires, which have been explained, all the transference of other passages is either from these sections or to them, except four clauses in doublets which have not been repeated in their proper place.

Second, while in the unbroken quires the doublets are few and almost always of a formal kind, like 'He that hath an ear', or 'voices and thunder and lightning', in these sheets they are extensive. Seeing that they are about as long as what is removed, it looks as though the doublets were meant as compensation.

As the writing material might not have been of the best, that quires should be broken might have happened even with a moderate amount of passing from hand to hand. But even the minimum use of the MS. necessary to effect such an accident is difficult to credit. Had the MS. been much read, there would have been people for the editor to appeal to for its order, and dissatisfied readers when he circulated his work. Moreover, the pages must have been mixed hopelessly as well as the quires broken. This is the more difficult that the other pages, in spite of being in broken quires, are in their right places.

The pages under discussion have a character which may be the explanation. §§ XI–XII plainly predict the overthrow of the Roman Empire and, in §§ XXIII–IV, we have the claim that the kingdom of Christ is to rise in its place. In § VI, though its language is somewhat veiled, we have an indication that the fuller treatment, which, according to the method of the book, would likely follow, may have been more explicit in its hostility to the Empire. Probably, therefore, the missing § VII made clearer than any other section what the book was.

§ XXVII, the misplacing of which causes the disorder in the last four sections, also speaks of reigning and judging.

The possible explanation, therefore, is that, for the safety of those having this book in their possession, these five or six pages were cut out.

§ VII, being much the most important and the most dangerous, may have been so securely hidden as never to be found again. The same cause might also explain why the order of the quires was altered. qq. 2–4 might well appear still too plain: and certainly the part now first is more general and, therefore, more innocuous. It would look like the ordinary Jewish literature of this type: and the expectation that no one but a Christian would trouble to read farther was probably well-founded.

There is also another possible supposition. If the original was written in Patmos, which—as "I was in Patmos" does not mean "was at a former time" but "I came to be"—there is no reason to question, the MS. would have to be sent out under the eyes of the Roman authorities. Censoring is not probably a modern invention. Would they have passed a book which said plainly that the Roman power would fall and the Christian replace it? But it would be much easier to smuggle out a few sheets than the whole book: and a page which was the key to the whole might have been sent by itself and have failed to arrive.

(*d*) *The Editor's* MS.

Though this explanation should be wholly incorrect, there can be little doubt that, for some reason, the MS. had been disarranged before it came into the hands of the editor.

On the supposition of quires, as given above, the probable order in which he found it was, using numerals for the quires and small letters for the pages, 1, 5, 6 (a, b), 7 (c, d, a, b, or possibly c absent), 2 (a, b, d), 3 (a, b), 4. Of q. 2, c was missing and of 3, c, d, and of 6, c, d, and possibly of 7, c or c, d, were by themselves and out of order.

First we shall deal with quire 7, because it has to do with the transposition both of the quires and of its own pages. This is §§ XXV–XXVIII.

As arranged by the editor c and d come before a and b. As part of d is put at the end, it might be supposed that the editor found it in its right place, and only transposed the pages because he had decided that the Holy Jerusalem must be the end, and that the Last Judgment must precede it.

But against this there are two arguments.

(*a*) If ch. xx. had followed xxii, he would have seen that the first part was in sequence, and have left it and not have transferred it to the Introduction.

(*b*) There is some evidence that quires 2–4 followed ch. xxii.

First, part of q. 2 is inserted into ch. xxii. True, this place was almost the only possible context, yet we must suppose that the place where it was put was under consideration at the time.

Again, if this supposed arrangement be correct, the end of the MS. as the editor found it was quire 4: and we find a reason why he begins to write after it the passage beginning with "These are the faithful and true words", xix. 9–10. This is that his first intention was not to transfer all q. 7 to the end, as he ultimately does, but only the closing part.

Finally, one of his separate pages follows as if it had puzzled the editor so completely that he simply put it last as an appendix, which also suggests that he had not then transferred q. 7 to the end.

Before beginning, he would naturally place the separate pages where he thought they belonged. He would know where the page in q. 2 was wanting, because only the inner sheet was divided, and p. c clearly went with p. d. But he did not know that it was the missing page, and inserted one which belonged elsewhere: and this error led to confusion about the others. Also, while he would know in which quires the other pages went, if both sheets were divided, he might not know whether these pages were missing before or after the other two.

Let us now suppose his quires in the order suggested. He thinks five seals are missing and four trumpets. The seals he probably takes to be the missing page. The plagues he takes to be the missing trumpets, so puts this page at the beginning of q. 6, which is the wrong place, as well as the wrong page. The next woe was overdue, so he enters the page with it in the vacant place in q. 2. Then he puts the other two in q. 3, where they are in the right place, but are the wrong pages.

When he comes to the page he starts on the vials as the trumpets, but he becomes doubtful, and, when he sees that he must also have seven vials, he begins to divide. After the third trumpet he fills up with darkening of the sun and moon from elsewhere, and then proceeds to look for the real place of the vials. The page he had put in in q.3 ends with angels with plagues, so he concludes that, as this also has plagues, it must be the second misplaced page of this quire. But then he has one he does not know what to do with, so he just puts it at the end of the book as it was then arranged.

But, when he had finished with the last woe, he discovered that the rest of his page went with the page in q.3. As the woe was already overdue, he did not remove it, but only put the rest with what followed it. This accounts for part of a section (ch. xi. 15–19) being separated from the rest.

Now we also see why he transfers so freely from and to these pages. They are separate and he can read them with any other page, and he is seeking in perplexity for their right connexion. This explains also why they are glossed, no longer only with mere memorable phrases, but with whole verses.

The chief perplexity which remains is to find some reason why so careful a scribe should repeat from his author at all, and especially so copiously. The most obvious suggestion is that, as he knew the original was seven double quires, he wished his copy to be the same. But the doublets are more than would compensate for the missing page.

Whether it be the explanation or not, I do not venture to say, but if we take the first doublet "He that hath an ear to hear, let him hear what the Spirit says to the Churches", and suppose that he entered it because it was of the exact length which made up either for his closer writing or his larger page, and that either this closer writing or this larger page runs throughout, and that the glosses are to compensate for it as well as the missing page, it works out as nearly exactly as possible. There are 27 pages of 34 lines and 32 lines more. But the doublet is a fraction short of a line, and $\frac{1}{14}$th would make exactly 28 pages of 34 lines minus $\frac{1}{14}$th.

This has also some confirmation from the fact that the pages up to the opening of the seals, if we balance what is omitted and added, are approximately 34 lines. Further, a good many doublets in the book are about the length of the first doublet. After the seals his doublets expand, which might be to make up for the missing sheet. Also, on this principle he seems to have made up pretty exactly to the end of ch. xi.

This is not offered as more than a possible suggestion, but it at least shows that the editor may have had some reason, even if this be not the right one, for thus expanding his text, which delivered him from the fear of the terrible curse for altering it.

X

THE BOOK AS A WHOLE

As the book is now arranged it consists of seven approximately equal parts:

I. The Messages to the Churches.

This now has its own conclusion and is apart from the rest. It is a prophecy of warning, and so is from a loud angel. The rest is concerned with God's deeds and is from a strong angel.

II. The Second Call with its roll of prophecy, and the origin in the Divine counsel of the World-order.

After the missing page we have the casting down from heaven of Satan and his angels. This seems to show that the origin of the World-order began with a scene in heaven, in a way parallel to the establishment of the God or Christ-rule.

If this be right, the missing page would have shed valuable light on the Jewish and Jewish-Christian ideas of the time, and it might have made some of the ideas in the book plainer.

III. The Calling up of the World-kingdom and the False Prophet, and Judgment upon them.

IV. The World-rule which is incarnated in them, and judgment upon it. In both cases, this is by what we may call natural calamities.

V. The Heavenly Council, and the opening of the roll of the Divine purpose of the new order.

VI. The Woes, which are a daimonic judgment and also a judgment upon the daimonic as well as the human sources of evil.

VII. The Holy Jerusalem and the Final State.

Though only the third and the last parts end exactly with what we have taken to be the quires, they approximately correspond with them.

The most perplexing part of the theology is the Spirit. He has no place at all in heaven. There we have only the seven spirits of God. He is introduced only three times, and each time in connexion with the Church or the Saints. In iii. 22 the churches are to hear what he says. In xiv. 13 the Spirit says that the saints rest from their labours and their works follow them. In xxii. 17 the Spirit and the Bride await Christ's coming. It is a question whether the Spirit is conceived personally at all, or whether we have not some abstract conception like the 'Bride', which is the Christ-rule.

Christ is essentially the Messiah, probably the eternal embodiment of this rule, and with him are associated the 144,000, whose names are written in his book of life from the foundation of the world.

Only once have we God called Father. Elsewhere it is "he who sits on the throne", and throne is the symbol and source of all righteous rule. We can only suppose that it comes from the teaching of Jesus, and that to the author it represents a special relation to the saints.

On the first part of the book the only change this introduces into the exposition in my previous work is that The Messages now have their definite conclusion, and my attempt to connect them with what follows is no longer required. The details of the exposition are not affected. In the latter part the change of order is considerable and affects very largely the whole general view, but it does not affect materially the details of the exposition. There is now quite definitely a second coming of an objective and catastrophic nature, but the Christ-rule seems even more clearly to be described in symbol, and to be no more a visible city than the World-rule. Also the final state is only a continuation of the Holy City: but there is something like Paul's view "Then shall he deliver up the kingdom to the Father".

In reading this book, and much more in the New Testament, much misunderstanding arises from taking the problem of the age for the pious Jew and Jewish Christian to be individual sin. What distressed and perplexed them was that anything so divisive and self-destructive as evil should be able to organise itself and rule in defiance of God. This seemed to require an organising mind: and hence the conception of Satan.

In the Gospels he is the prince of this world as much as in Revelation. In the Lord's prayer, it is not "Deliver us from evil", but "from the evil one". The supreme choice for men is not between evil actions and good alone or even primarily, but between the kingdom of Satan and the kingdom of God. Of devotion to the former the essential aspect is the idolatry of might as embodied in the world-kingdoms, and of the latter the worship of service as embodied in the Lamb.

The book of Revelation, therefore, does not begin with the origin of evil. This is not ascribed to Satan. It begins with the organisation of evil into world-dominion. So far is this from being the beginning of evil that it is the beginning of its final defeat. The fall of Satan and his angels only organises evil in the earth as a sort of last ditch in the spiritual conflict.

Even in the Christ-rule, however, evil is not at an end. On the contrary, it remains so that all that is not wholly obdurate may be won by good before the final judgment. The difference is that now it is good that has one head, is organised to rule, and can win for itself all that is not obdurately committed to iniquity.

Note. The text which follows is printed in two types. This was merely copied from Gebhardt by the printer and has no significance. Gebhardt's line might have some importance, but it has not been very accurately reproduced, because a good English printer spaces by a sense of the general effect and dislikes dividing words except in certain definite ways. This, I think, is the chief reason why an English text seems to be a less accurate standard than a German for an evenly written MS. with no spaces and with the line ending at any syllable. The average of a long page, however, would be more precise than lines, so the important point is, that, by a standard before determined, the length of the sections is in every case exactly equal.

PART II

TEXT AND TRANSLATION

§ I

Ch. i. 9—ii. 3

9 Ἐγὼ Ἰωάννης, ὁ ἀδελφὸς ὑμῶν καὶ συνκοινωνὸς ἐν τῇ θλίψει καὶ βασιλείᾳ καὶ ὑπομονῇ ἐν Ἰησοῦ, ἐγενόμην ἐν τῇ νήσῳ τῇ καλουμένῃ Πάτμῳ διὰ τὸν λόγον τοῦ θεοῦ καὶ διὰ τὴν μαρτυρίαν Ἰησοῦ. 10 ἐγενόμην ἐν πνεύματι ἐν τῇ κυριακῇ ἡμέρᾳ, καὶ ἤκουσα ὀπίσω μου φωνὴν μεγάλην ὡς σάλπιγγος 11 λεγούσης· ὃ βλέπεις γράψον εἰς βιβλίον καὶ πέμψον ταῖς ἑπτὰ ἐκκλησίαις, εἰς Ἔφεσον καὶ εἰς Ζμύρναν καὶ εἰς Πέργαμον καὶ εἰς Θυάτειρα καὶ εἰς Σάρδεις καὶ εἰς Φιλαδελφίαν καὶ εἰς Λαοδικίαν. 12 καὶ ἐπέστρεψα βλέπειν τὴν φωνὴν ἥτις ἐλάλει μετ' ἐμοῦ· καὶ ἐπιστρέψας εἶδον ἑπτὰ λυχνίας χρυσᾶς, 13 καὶ ἐν μέσῳ τῶν λυχνιῶν ὅμοιον υἱὸν ἀνθρώπου, ἐνδεδυμένον ποδήρη καὶ περιεζωσμένον πρὸς τοῖς μασθοῖς ζώνην χρυσᾶν· 14 ἡ δὲ κεφαλὴ αὐτοῦ καὶ αἱ τρίχες λευκαὶ ὡς ἔριον λευκὸν ὡς χιών, καὶ οἱ ὀφθαλμοὶ αὐτοῦ ὡς φλὸξ πυρός, 15 καὶ οἱ πόδες αὐτοῦ ὅμοιοι χαλκολιβάνῳ ὡς ἐν καμίνῳ πεπυρωμένῳ, καὶ ἡ φωνὴ αὐτοῦ ὡς φωνὴ ὑδάτων πολλῶν, 16 καὶ ἔχων ἐν τῇ δεξιᾷ χειρὶ αὐτοῦ ἀστέρας ἑπτά, καὶ ἐκ τοῦ στόματος αὐτοῦ ῥομφαία δίστομος ὀξεῖα ἐκπορευομένη, καὶ ἡ ὄψις αὐτοῦ ὡς ὁ ἥλιος φαίνει ἐν τῇ δυνάμει αὐτοῦ. 17 καὶ ὅτε εἶδον αὐτόν, ἔπεσα πρὸς τοὺς πόδας αὐτοῦ ὡς νεκρός, καὶ ἔθηκεν τὴν δεξιὰν αὐτοῦ ἐπ' ἐμὲ λέγων· μὴ φοβοῦ· ἐγώ εἰμι ὁ πρῶτος καὶ ὁ ἔσχατος 18 καὶ ὁ ζῶν, καὶ ἐγενόμην νεκρὸς καὶ ἰδοὺ ζῶν εἰμὶ εἰς τοὺς αἰῶνας τῶν αἰώνων, καὶ ἔχω τὰς κλεῖς τοῦ θανάτου καὶ τοῦ ᾅδου. 19 γράψον οὖν ἃ εἶδες καὶ ἃ εἰσὶν καὶ ἃ μέλλει γενέσθαι μετὰ ταῦτα, 20 τὸ μυστήριον τῶν ἑπτὰ ἀστέρων οὓς εἶδες ἐπὶ τῆς δεξιᾶς μου, καὶ τὰς ἑπτὰ λυχνίας τὰς χρυσᾶς. οἱ ἑπτὰ ἀστέρες ἄγγελοι τῶν ἑπτὰ ἐκκλησιῶν εἰσίν, καὶ αἱ λυχνίαι αἱ ἑπτὰ ἑπτὰ ἐκκλησίαι εἰσίν. 1 Τῷ ἀγγέλῳ τῆς ἐν Ἐφέσῳ ἐκκλησίας γράψον· τάδε λέγει ὁ κρατῶν τοὺς ἑπτὰ ἀστέρας ἐν τῇ δεξιᾷ αὐτοῦ, ὁ περιπατῶν ἐν μέσῳ τῶν ἑπτὰ λυχνιῶν τῶν χρυσῶν· 2 οἶδα τὰ ἔργα σου καὶ τὸν κόπον καὶ τὴν ὑπομονήν σου, καὶ ὅτι οὐ δύνῃ βαστάσαι κακούς, καὶ ἐπείρασας τοὺς λέγοντας ἑαυτοὺς ἀποστόλους καὶ οὐκ εἰσίν, καὶ εὗρες αὐτοὺς ψευδεῖς· 3 καὶ ὑπομονὴν ἔχεις, καὶ ἐβάστασας διὰ τὸ ὄνομά

§ I

The Prophetic Call

i. 9 I John, your brother and comrade, in the oppression and dominion and the patience which is in Jesus, came to be in the island called Patmos on account of God's word and the witness of Jesus. 10 I was in the spirit on the Lord's day and heard behind me a great voice, as of a trumpet[1], 11 saying: What thou seest write in a book and send to the seven churches—to Ephesus and to Smyrna and to Pergamum and to Thyatira and to Sardis and to Philadelphia and to Laodicea. 12 And I turned to see the voice which spake with me. And having turned I saw seven golden lampstands, 13 and amid the lampstands one like a Son of Man, clothed to His feet, and girded about the breasts with a golden girdle, 14 His head and His hair white like snow-white wool, His eyes as a flame of fire, 15 His feet like fine brass refined in a furnace; His voice like the voice of many waters[2]. 16 And He was holding in His right hand seven stars; from His mouth went out a sharp two-edged sword; and His countenance was as the sun shining in its might. 17 And when I saw Him I fell before His feet as one dead. But He placed His right hand upon me, saying: Fear not, I am the first and the last, 18 and the living one. I died, but behold I am living to ages of ages, and have the keys of death and of hades. 19 Write what thou hast seen—the things which are and the things about to be hereafter, 20 even the mystery of the seven stars which thou hast seen in my right hand, and the seven golden lampstands. The seven stars are the angels of the seven churches, and the seven lamps are the seven churches. ii. 1 To the angel of the church in Ephesus write: These things says He who holds the seven stars in His right hand, He who walks amid the seven golden lampstands: 2 I know thy works and thy suffering and thy patience and that thou canst not endure evil-doers, but hast tested those calling themselves apostles and are not, and hast found them false. 3 And thou hast patience and hast endured on account of My name and not

[1] Is. lviii. 1. Lift up thy voice like a trumpet. [2] Dan. vii. 9 and 13, 14. One that was ancient of days...his raiment was white as snow and the hair of his head like pure wool; his throne was fiery flame...one like unto a Son of man, and there was given him dominion and glory and a kingdom. x. 5, 6. A man clothed in linen, whose loins were girded with pure gold of Uphaz...his face as the appearance of lightning and his eyes as lamps of fire, his arms and feet like in colour to burnished brass, and the voice of his words as the voice of a multitude. Ez. i. 24. The noise of many waters.

§ II

CH. ii. 3–19

μου, καὶ οὐ κεκοπίακες. 4 ἀλλὰ ἔχω κατὰ σοῦ ὅτι τὴν ἀγάπην σου τὴν πρώτην ἀφῆκες. 5 μνημόνευε οὖν πόθεν πέπτωκες, καὶ μετανόησον καὶ τὰ πρῶτα ἔργα ποίησον· εἰ δὲ μή, ἔρχομαί σοι καὶ κινήσω τὴν λυχνίαν σου ἐκ τοῦ τόπου αὐτῆς, ἐὰν μὴ μετανοήσῃς. 6 ἀλλὰ τοῦτο ἔχεις, ὅτι μισεῖς τὰ ἔργα τῶν Νικολαϊτῶν, ἃ κἀγὼ μισῶ. 7 * τῷ νικῶντι δώσω αὐτῷ φαγεῖν ἐκ τοῦ ξύλου τῆς ζωῆς, ὅ ἐστιν ἐν τῷ παραδείσῳ τοῦ θεοῦ. 8 καὶ τῷ ἀγγέλῳ τῆς ἐν Ζμύρνῃ ἐκκλησίας γράψον· τάδε λέγει ὁ πρῶτος καὶ ὁ ἔσχατος, ὃς ἐγένετο νεκρὸς καὶ ἔζησεν· 9 οἶδά σου τὴν θλίψιν καὶ τὴν πτωχείαν, ἀλλὰ πλούσιος εἶ, καὶ τὴν βλασφημίαν ἐκ τῶν λεγόντων Ἰουδαίους εἶναι ἑαυτούς, καὶ οὐκ εἰσὶν ἀλλὰ συναγωγὴ τοῦ σατανᾶ. 10 μηδὲν φοβοῦ ἃ μέλλεις πάσχειν. ἰδοὺ μέλλει βάλλειν ὁ διάβολος ἐξ ὑμῶν εἰς φυλακὴν ἵνα πειρασθῆτε, καὶ ἕξετε θλίψιν ἡμερῶν δέκα. γίνου πιστὸς ἄχρι θανάτου, καὶ δώσω σοι τὸν στέφανον τῆς ζωῆς. 11 * ὁ νικῶν οὐ μὴ ἀδικηθῇ ἐκ τοῦ θανάτου τοῦ δευτέρου. 12 καὶ τῷ ἀγγέλῳ τῆς ἐν Περγάμῳ ἐκκλησίας γράψον· τάδε λέγει ὁ ἔχων τὴν ῥομφαίαν τὴν δίστομον τὴν ὀξεῖαν· 13 οἶδα ποῦ κατοικεῖς· ὅπου ὁ θρόνος τοῦ σατανᾶ· καὶ κρατεῖς τὸ ὄνομά μου, καὶ οὐκ ἠρνήσω τὴν πίστιν μου ἐν ταῖς ἡμέραις Ἀντείπας ὁ μάρτυς μου ὁ πιστός μου, ὃς ἀπεκτάνθη παρ' ὑμῖν, ὅπου ὁ σατανᾶς κατοικεῖ. 14 ἀλλ' ἔχω κατὰ σοῦ ὀλίγα, ὅτι ἔχεις ἐκεῖ κρατοῦντας τὴν διδαχὴν Βαλαάμ, ὃς ἐδίδασκεν τῷ Βαλὰκ βαλεῖν σκάνδαλον ἐνώπιον τῶν υἱῶν Ἰσραήλ, φαγεῖν εἰδωλόθυτα καὶ πορνεῦσαι. 15 οὕτως ἔχεις καὶ σὺ κρατοῦντας τὴν διδαχὴν τῶν Νικολαϊτῶν ὁμοίως. 16 μετανόησον· εἰ δὲ μή, ἔρχομαί σοι ταχὺ καὶ πολεμήσω μετ' αὐτῶν ἐν τῇ ῥομφαίᾳ τοῦ στόματός μου. 17 * τῷ νικοῦντι δώσω αὐτῷ τοῦ μάννα τοῦ κεκρυμμένου, καὶ δώσω αὐτῷ ψῆφον λευκήν, καὶ ἐπὶ τὴν ψῆφον ὄνομα καινὸν γεγραμμένον, ὃ οὐδεὶς οἶδεν εἰ μὴ ὁ λαμβάνων. 18 καὶ τῷ ἀγγέλῳ τῆς ἐν Θυατείροις ἐκκλησίας γράψον· τάδε λέγει ὁ υἱὸς τοῦ θεοῦ, ὁ ἔχων τοὺς ὀφθαλμοὺς αὐτοῦ ὡς φλὸξ πυρός, καὶ οἱ πόδες αὐτοῦ ὅμοιοι χαλκολιβάνῳ· 19 οἶδά σου τὰ ἔργα καὶ τὴν ἀγάπην καὶ τὴν πίστιν καὶ τὴν διακονίαν καὶ τὴν ὑπομονήν,

Asterisks indicate omissions, brackets restorations.

§ II

Ephesus, Smyrna, Pergamum, Thyatira

ii. 3 grown weary. 4 But I have against thee that thou hast left thy first love. 5 Remember, therefore, whence thou hast fallen, and repent and do the first works. If not, if thou repent not, I am coming to thee and will remove thy lampstand from its place. 6 Yet this thou hast that thou hatest the works of the Nicolaitans, which I also hate. 7 To the victor I will give to eat from the tree of life which is in the paradise of God. 8 And to the angel of the church in Smyrna write: These things says the first and the last[1], who was dead and came to life. 9 I know thy oppression and thy poverty, yet thou art rich; also the blasphemy of some who call themselves Jews, and are not, but are a synagogue of Satan. 10 Fear not what thou art going to suffer. Behold the devil is going to cast some of you into prison, that ye may be tried, and ye shall have oppression ten days[2]. Be faithful unto death and I will give thee the crown of life. 11 The victor shall not be hurt of the second death. 12 And to the angel of the church in Pergamum write: These things says He who has the sharp two-edged sword. 13 I know where thou dwellest, where is Satan's throne. Yet thou holdest fast My name, and didst not deny My faith in the days of Antipas, My witness, My faithful one, who was put to death among you where Satan dwells. 14 Yet I have somewhat against thee, that thou hast there those who hold the teaching of Balaam who taught Balak to put a stumbling-block before the children of Israel, to eat idol-offerings and commit fornication. 15 In like manner too thou hast those who hold the teaching of the Nicolaitans. 16 Repent: if not, I am coming to thee soon and will war against them with the sword of My mouth[3]. 17 To the victor I will give of the hidden manna; and I will give him a white stone, and on the stone a new name written which no one knows save the receiver. 18 And to the angel of the church in Thyatira write: These things says the Son of God who has His eyes as a flame of fire, and His feet are like fine brass. 19 I know thy works, and thy love, and thy faith, and thy service,

[1] Is. xli. 4. I the Lord, the first, and with the last, I am he. [2] Dan. xi. 33. Yet they shall fall by the sword and by flame, by captivity and by spoil *for* days. [3] Is. xlix. 2. He hath made my mouth like a sharp sword.

§ III

Ch. ii. 19—iii. 7

καὶ τὰ ἔργα σου τὰ ἔσχατα πλείονα τῶν πρώτων. 20 ἀλλ' ἔχω κατὰ σοῦ ὅτι ἀφεῖς τὴν γυναῖκα Ἰεζάβελ, ἡ λέγουσα αὐτὴν προφῆτιν καὶ διδάσκει καὶ πλανᾷ τοὺς ἐμοὺς δούλους πορνεῦσαι καὶ φαγεῖν εἰδωλόθυτα. 21 καὶ ἔδωκα αὐτῇ χρόνον ἵνα μετανοήσῃ, καὶ οὐ θέλει μετανοῆσαι ἐκ τῆς πορνείας αὐτῆς. 22 ἰδοὺ βάλλω αὐτὴν εἰς κλίνην, καὶ τοὺς μοιχεύοντας μετ' αὐτῆς εἰς θλίψιν μεγάλην, ἐὰν μὴ μετανοήσουσιν ἐκ τῶν ἔργων αὐτῆς. 23 καὶ τὰ τέκνα αὐτῆς ἀποκτενῶ ἐν θανάτῳ, καὶ γνώσονται πᾶσαι αἱ ἐκκλησίαι ὅτι ἐγώ εἰμι ὁ ἐραυνῶν νεφροὺς καὶ καρδίας, καὶ δώσω ὑμῖν ἑκάστῳ κατὰ τὰ ἔργα ὑμῶν. 24 ὑμῖν δὲ λέγω τοῖς λοιποῖς τοῖς ἐν Θυατείροις, ὅσοι οὐκ ἔχουσιν τὴν διδαχὴν ταύτην, οἵτινες οὐκ ἔγνωσαν τὰ βαθέα τοῦ σατανᾶ, ὡς λέγουσιν· οὐ βάλλω ἐφ' ὑμᾶς ἄλλο βάρος· 25 πλὴν ὃ ἔχετε κρατήσατε ἄχρι οὗ ἂν ἥξω. 26 καὶ ὁ νικῶν καὶ ὁ τηρῶν ἄχρι τέλους τὰ ἔργα μου, δώσω αὐτῷ ἐξουσίαν ἐπὶ τῶν ἐθνῶν, 27 καὶ ποιμανεῖ αὐτοὺς ἐν ῥάβδῳ σιδηρᾷ, ὡς τὰ σκεύη τὰ κεραμικὰ συντρίβεται, ὡς κἀγὼ εἴληφα παρὰ τοῦ πατρός μου, 28 καὶ δώσω αὐτῷ τὸν ἀστέρα τὸν πρωϊνόν. *1 καὶ τῷ ἀγγέλῳ τῆς ἐν Σάρδεσιν ἐκκλησίας γράψον· τάδε λέγει ὁ ἔχων τὰ ἑπτὰ πνεύματα τοῦ θεοῦ καὶ τοὺς ἑπτὰ ἀστέρας· οἶδά σου τὰ ἔργα, ὅτι ὄνομα ἔχεις ὅτι ζῇς, καὶ νεκρὸς εἶ. 2 γίνου γρηγορῶν, καὶ στήρισον τὰ λοιπὰ ἃ ἔμελλον ἀποθανεῖν. οὐ γὰρ εὕρηκά σου τὰ ἔργα πεπληρωμένα ἐνώπιον τοῦ θεοῦ μου. 3 μνημόνευε οὖν πῶς εἴληφας καὶ ἤκουσας, καὶ τήρει καὶ μετανόησον. ἐὰν οὖν μὴ γρηγορήσῃς, ἥξω ὡς κλέπτης, καὶ οὐ μὴ γνώσῃ ποίαν ὥραν ἥξω ἐπὶ σέ. 4 ἀλλὰ ἔχεις ὀλίγα ὀνόματα ἐν Σάρδεσιν ἃ οὐκ ἐμόλυναν τὰ ἱμάτια αὐτῶν, καὶ περιπατήσουσιν μετ' ἐμοῦ ἐν λευκοῖς, ὅτι ἄξιοί εἰσιν. 5 ὁ νικῶν οὕτως περιβαλεῖται ἐν ἱματίοις λευκοῖς, καὶ οὐ μὴ ἐξαλείψω τὸ ὄνομα αὐτοῦ ἐκ τῆς βίβλου τῆς ζωῆς, καὶ ὁμολογήσω τὸ ὄνομα αὐτοῦ ἐνώπιον τοῦ πατρός μου καὶ ἐνώπιον τῶν ἀγγέλων αὐτοῦ.* 7 καὶ τῷ ἀγγέλῳ τῆς ἐν Φιλαδελφίᾳ ἐκκλησίας γράψον· τάδε λέγει ὁ ἅγιος ὁ ἀληθινός, ὁ ἔχων τὴν κλεῖν τοῦ Δαυείδ, ὁ ἀνοίγων καὶ οὐδεὶς κλείσει, καὶ κλείων καὶ οὐδεὶς ἀνοίξει·

§ III

THYATIRA, SARDIS

ii. 19 and thy patience and thy works—the last more than the first. 20 But I have against thee that thou permittest the woman Jezebel, who calls herself a prophetess, while she teaches, yea deludes My servants into committing fornication and eating idol-offerings. 21 I gave her time that she might repent: but she wishes not to repent of her fornication. 22 Lo I cast her into a bed, and those who commit fornication with her into great trial, except they repent of their works. 23 And her children I will slay with pestilence. Thus all the churches shall know that it is I who am examining reins and hearts, and I will award to each of you in accord with your works. 24 I say to the rest of you in Thyatira—those who have not this teaching, whosoever know not the depths of Satan as they say—I lay not on you any other burden: 25 only what you have hold fast till I shall come. 26 But to the victor who holds fast My works to the end I will give power over the nations, 27 and he shall shepherd them with an iron rod, as earthenware vessels are shivered. As I Myself have received of My Father, 28 I will give him the morning star. iii. 1 And to the angel of the church in Sardis write: These things says He who has the seven spirits of God and the seven stars. I know thy works, that thou hast a reputation of being alive, but art dead. 2 Become awake and brace up what remains and was about to die. For I have not found thy tasks fulfilled before My God. 3 Recall then how thou hast received and heard, and hold fast and repent. But if thou be not on watch, I will come as a thief, and thou shalt not know what hour I will come on thee. 4 Yet thou hast a few persons in Sardis who have not defiled their garments, and they shall walk with Me in white because they are worthy. 5 Thus the victor shall be clothed in white garments, and I will never blot his name out of the book of life, but will acknowledge his name before My Father and before His angels. 7 And to the angel of the church in Philadelphia write: These things says the holy, the true, the possessor of the key of David, He who opens and no one shall shut, and shuts and no one shall open[1].

[1] Is. xxii. 22. And the key of David I will lay upon his shoulder; and he shall open and none shall shut; and he shall shut and none shall open. Mt. xvi. 18. For the relation of this to the gates of Hades (Rev. i. 18) and the keys of the kingdom of heaven.

§ IV

Ch. iii. 8–22

8 οἶδά σου τὰ ἔργα· ἰδοὺ δέδωκα ἐνώπιόν σου θύραν ἠνεῳγμένην, ἣν οὐδεὶς δύναται κλεῖσαι αὐτήν· ὅτι μικρὰν ἔχεις δύναμιν, καὶ ἐτήρησάς μου τὸν λόγον καὶ οὐκ ἠρνήσω τὸ ὄνομά μου. 9 ἰδοὺ διδῶ ἐκ τῆς συναγωγῆς τοῦ σατανᾶ τῶν λεγόντων ἑαυτοὺς Ἰουδαίους εἶναι, καὶ οὐκ εἰσὶν ἀλλὰ ψεύδονται· ἰδοὺ ποιήσω αὐτοὺς ἵνα ἥξουσιν καὶ προσκυνήσουσιν ἐνώπιον τῶν ποδῶν σου, καὶ γνῶσιν ὅτι ἐγὼ ἠγάπησά σε. 10 ὅτι ἐτήρησας τὸν λόγον τῆς ὑπομονῆς μου, κἀγώ σε τηρήσω ἐκ τῆς ὥρας τοῦ πειρασμοῦ τῆς μελλούσης ἔρχεσθαι ἐπὶ τῆς οἰκουμένης ὅλης, πειράσαι τοὺς κατοικοῦντας ἐπὶ τῆς γῆς. 11 ἔρχομαι ταχύ· κράτει ὃ ἔχεις, ἵνα μηδεὶς λάβῃ τὸν στέφανόν σου. 12 ὁ νικῶν, ποιήσω αὐτὸν στῦλον ἐν τῷ ναῷ τοῦ θεοῦ μου, καὶ ἔξω οὐ μὴ ἐξέλθῃ ἔτι, καὶ γράψω ἐπ' αὐτὸν τὸ ὄνομα τοῦ θεοῦ μου καὶ τὸ ὄνομα τῆς πόλεως τοῦ θεοῦ μου, τῆς καινῆς Ἱερουσαλὴμ ἡ καταβαίνουσα ἐκ τοῦ οὐρανοῦ ἀπὸ τοῦ θεοῦ μου, καὶ τὸ ὄνομά μου τὸ καινόν. * 14 καὶ τῷ ἀγγέλῳ τῆς ἐν Λαοδικίᾳ ἐκκλησίας γράψον· τάδε λέγει ὁ ἀμήν, ὁ μάρτυς ὁ πιστὸς καὶ ἀληθινός, ἡ ἀρχὴ τῆς κτίσεως τοῦ θεοῦ· 15 οἶδά σου τὰ ἔργα, ὅτι οὔτε ψυχρὸς εἶ οὔτε ζεστός. ὄφελον ψυχρὸς ἦς ἢ ζεστός. 16 οὕτως ὅτι χλιαρὸς εἶ, καὶ οὔτε ζεστὸς οὔτε ψυχρός, μέλλω σε ἐμέσαι ἐκ τοῦ στόματός μου. 17 ὅτι λέγεις ὅτι πλούσιός εἰμι καὶ πεπλούτηκα καὶ οὐδὲν χρείαν ἔχω, καὶ οὐκ οἶδας ὅτι σὺ εἶ ὁ ταλαίπωρος καὶ ἐλεεινὸς καὶ πτωχὸς καὶ τυφλὸς καὶ γυμνός, 18 συμβουλεύω σοι ἀγοράσαι παρ' ἐμοῦ χρυσίον πεπυρωμένον ἐκ πυρὸς ἵνα πλουτήσῃς, καὶ ἱμάτια λευκὰ ἵνα περιβάλῃ καὶ μὴ φανερωθῇ ἡ αἰσχύνη τῆς γυμνότητός σου, καὶ κολλύριον ἔγχρισαι τοὺς ὀφθαλμούς σου ἵνα βλέπῃς. 19 ἐγὼ ὅσους ἐὰν φιλῶ ἐλέγχω καὶ παιδεύω· ζήλευε οὖν καὶ μετανόησον. 20 ἰδοὺ ἕστηκα ἐπὶ τὴν θύραν καὶ κρούω· ἐάν τις ἀκούσῃ τῆς φωνῆς μου καὶ ἀνοίξῃ τὴν θύραν, καὶ εἰσελεύσομαι πρὸς αὐτὸν καὶ δειπνήσω μετ' αὐτοῦ καὶ αὐτὸς μετ' ἐμοῦ. 21 ὁ νικῶν, δώσω αὐτῷ καθίσαι μετ' ἐμοῦ ἐν τῷ θρόνῳ μου, ὡς κἀγὼ ἐνίκησα καὶ ἐκάθισα μετὰ τοῦ πατρός μου ἐν τῷ θρόνῳ αὐτοῦ. 22 ὁ ἔχων οὖς ἀκουσάτω τί τὸ πνεῦμα λέγει ταῖς ἐκκλησίαις.

§ IV

PHILADELPHIA, LAODICEA

iii. 8 I know thy works. Lo, I have set an open door before thee, which no one can shut: because thou hast some little strength and hast held fast My word and not denied My name. 9 Lo, I will give some from the synagogue of Satan, of those who say they are Jews and are not, but lie—lo, I will make them come and kneel before thy feet, that they may know that I have loved thee. 10 Because thou hast kept the word of My patience, I also will keep thee from the hour of trial which is about to come on the whole civilised world to try those dwelling on the earth. 11 I come quickly. Hold fast what thou hast that no one take away thy crown. 12 The victor will I make a pillar in the temple of My God, and outside he shall never more go. And I will write on him the name of My God and the name of the city of My God—the new Jerusalem which comes down out of heaven from My God, and My name, the new one. 14 And to the angel of the church in Laodicea write: These things says the Amen, the faithful and true Witness, the beginning of the creation of God. 15 I know thy works, that thou art neither cold nor hot. Would thou wert cold or hot! 16 So, as thou art luke-warm, and neither cold nor hot, I will spue thee out of My mouth. 17 Because thou sayest, I am rich, I have been enriched and have no want, and dost not know that thou art miserable, pitiable, poor, blind and naked, 18 I counsel thee to buy from Me gold purified in the fire that thou mayest be rich, and white raiment that thou mayest be clothed and the shame of thy nakedness may not appear, and to anoint with eye-salve thine eyes that thou mayest see. 19 Those I love I rebuke and chasten. Have zeal then and repent. 20 Lo, I stand at the door and knock. If any one hear My voice and open the door, I will come in to him and sup with him, and he with Me. 21 To the victor I will grant to sit with Me on My throne, even as I was victorious and sat down with My Father on His throne. 22 He who has ears to hear, let him hear what the Spirit says to the churches.

§ V

Ch. xxii. 10–12, x. 1–11

10 (καὶ λέγει μοι· μὴ σφραγίσῃς τοὺς λόγους τῆς προφητείας τοῦ βιβλίου τούτου· ὁ καιρὸς γὰρ ἐγγύς ἐστιν. 11 ὁ ἀδικῶν ἀδικησάτω ἔτι, καὶ ὁ ῥυπαρὸς ῥυπανθήτω ἔτι, καὶ ὁ δίκαιος δικαιοσύνην ποιησάτω ἔτι, καὶ ὁ ἅγιος ἁγιασθήτω ἔτι. 12 ἰδοὺ ἔρχομαι ταχύ, καὶ ὁ μισθός μου μετ' ἐμοῦ, ἀποδοῦναι ἑκάστῳ ὡς τὸ ἔργον ἐστὶν αὐτοῦ.) 1 Καὶ εἶδον ἄλλον ἄγγελον ἰσχυρὸν καταβαίνοντα ἐκ τοῦ οὐρανοῦ, περιβεβλημένον νεφέλην, καὶ ἡ ἶρις ἐπὶ τὴν κεφαλὴν αὐτοῦ, καὶ τὸ πρόσωπον αὐτοῦ ὡς ὁ ἥλιος, καὶ οἱ πόδες αὐτοῦ ὡς στῦλοι πυρός, 2 καὶ ἔχων ἐν τῇ χειρὶ αὐτοῦ βιβλαρίδιον ἠνεῳγμένον. καὶ ἔθηκεν τὸν πόδα αὐτοῦ τὸν δεξιὸν ἐπὶ τῆς θαλάσσης, τὸν δὲ εὐώνυμον ἐπὶ τῆς γῆς, 3 καὶ ἔκραξεν φωνῇ μεγάλῃ ὥσπερ λέων μυκᾶται. καὶ ὅτε ἔκραξεν, ἐλάλησαν αἱ ἑπτὰ βρονταὶ τὰς ἑαυτῶν φωνάς. 4 καὶ ὅτε ἐλάλησαν αἱ ἑπτὰ βρονταί, ἔμελλον γράφειν, καὶ ἤκουσα φωνὴν ἐκ τοῦ οὐρανοῦ λέγουσαν· σφράγισον ἃ ἐλάλησαν αἱ ἑπτὰ βρονταί, καὶ μὴ αὐτὰ γράψῃς. 5 καὶ ὁ ἄγγελος, ὃν εἶδον ἑστῶτα ἐπὶ τῆς θαλάσσης καὶ ἐπὶ τῆς γῆς, ἦρεν τὴν χεῖρα αὐτοῦ τὴν δεξιὰν εἰς τὸν οὐρανόν, 6 καὶ ὤμοσεν ἐν τῷ ζῶντι εἰς τοὺς αἰῶνας τῶν αἰώνων, ὃς ἔκτισεν τὸν οὐρανὸν καὶ τὰ ἐν αὐτῷ καὶ τὴν γῆν καὶ τὰ ἐν αὐτῇ καὶ τὴν θάλασσαν καὶ τα ἐν αὐτῇ, ὅτι χρόνος οὐκέτι ἔσται, 7 ἀλλ' ἐν ταῖς ἡμέραις τῆς φωνῆς τοῦ ἑβδόμου ἀγγέλου, ὅταν μέλλῃ σαλπίζειν, καὶ ἐτελέσθη τὸ μυστήριον τοῦ θεοῦ, ὡς εὐηγγέλισεν τοὺς ἑαυτοῦ δούλους τοὺς προφήτας. 8 καὶ ἡ φωνὴ ἣν ἤκουσα ἐκ τοῦ οὐρανοῦ πάλιν λαλοῦσαν μετ' ἐμοῦ καὶ λέγουσαν· ὕπαγε λάβε τὸ βιβλαρίδιον τὸ ἠνεῳγμένον ἐν τῇ χειρὶ τοῦ ἀγγέλου τοῦ ἑστῶτος ἐπὶ τῆς θαλάσσης καὶ ἐπὶ τῆς γῆς. 9 καὶ ἀπῆλθα πρὸς τὸν ἄγγελον, λέγων αὐτῷ δοῦναί μοι τὸ βιβλαρίδιον. καὶ λέγει μοι· λάβε καὶ κατάφαγε αὐτό, καὶ πικρανεῖ σου τὴν κοιλίαν, ἀλλ' ἐν τῷ στόματί σου ἔσται γλυκὺ ὡς μέλι. 10 καὶ ἔλαβον τὸ βιβλαρίδιον ἐκ τῆς χειρὸς τοῦ ἀγγέλου καὶ κατέφαγον αὐτό, καὶ ἦν ἐν τῷ στόματί μου ὡς μέλι γλυκύ· καὶ ὅτε ἔφαγον αὐτό, ἐπικράνθη ἡ κοιλία μου. * 11 καὶ λέγουσίν μοι· δεῖ σε πάλιν προφητεῦσαι ἐπὶ λαοῖς καὶ ἔθνεσιν καὶ γλώσσαις καὶ βασιλεῦσιν πολλοῖς.

§ V

Second Prophetic Call

xxii. 10 Then he says to me: Seal not up the words of the prophecy of this roll for the time is near. 11 Let the unjust be unjust still, and the filthy be filthy still, but let the righteous do righteousness still, and the holy be holy still[1]. 12 Lo I come quickly and my reward is with me, to render to each as his work is. x. 1 Then I saw, coming down out of heaven, another angel—a strong one. He was cloud-enfolded, the rainbow over his head[2], his face as the sun and his feet as pillars of fire[3], 2 and in his hand he held a small open roll[4]. He set his right foot on the sea and his left on the land, 3 and he cried with a great voice as a lion roars[5]. And, when he cried, the seven thunders spake forth their voices[6]. 4 And, when the seven thunders had spoken, I was about to write. But I heard a voice from heaven saying: Seal up what things the seven thunders have spoken and write them not. 5 And the angel whom I saw standing on the sea and on the land lifted up his right hand towards heaven, 6 and swore by him who lives to ages of ages, who created the heavens and what is therein, the earth and what is therein, and the sea and what is therein, that there shall be no more delay, 7 but, in the days of the voice of the seventh angel, when he is to sound his trumpet, then God's mystery shall be ended, as He has given His servants the prophets the good-news. 8 Then the voice which I heard from heaven was again speaking unto me, saying: Go, take the small roll which is open in the hand of the angel standing on the sea and on the land. 9 Then I went to the angel, saying to him: Give me the small roll; and he says to me: Take and eat it; and it will make bitter thy belly, though in thy mouth it will be sweet as honey. 10 And I took the small roll from the hand of the angel and ate it up. And it was in my mouth sweet as honey, but when I ate it my belly was embittered[7]. 11 And they say to me: It is required that thou also shouldest prophesy again concerning many peoples and nations and tongues and kings.

[1] Dan. xii. 10. Many shall purify themselves...but the wicked shall do wickedly. [2] Ez. i. 28. As the appearance of the bow that is in the cloud in the day of rain, so was the appearance of the brightness round about. This was the appearance of the likeness of the glory of the Lord. [3] Ez. i. 27. And from the appearance of his loins downward I saw as it were the appearance of fire. [4] Ez. ii. 9. An hand was put forth unto me; and lo a roll of a book was therein. [5] Amos iii. 8. The lion roars, who will not fear? The Lord God hath spoken, who can but prophesy? [6] Ez. ii. 10. And there was written therein lamentations and mourning and woe. [7] Ez. iii. 1. Eat this roll and go speak unto the house of Israel....Fill thy bowels with this roll that I give thee. Then did I eat it; and it was in my mouth as honey for sweetness. *v.* 14. And I went in bitterness.

§ VI

Ch. xi. 1–13

1 Καὶ ἐδόθη μοι κάλαμος ὅμοιος ῥάβδῳ, λέγων· ἔγειρε καὶ μέτρησον τὸν ναὸν τοῦ θεοῦ καὶ τὸ θυσιαστήριον καὶ τοὺς προσκυνοῦντας ἐν αὐτῷ. 2 καὶ τὴν αὐλὴν τὴν ἔξωθεν τοῦ ναοῦ ἔκβαλε ἔξωθεν καὶ μὴ αὐτὴν μετρήσῃς, ὅτι ἐδόθη τοῖς ἔθνεσιν, καὶ τὴν πόλιν τὴν ἁγίαν πατήσουσιν μῆνας τεσσεράκοντα δύο. 3 καὶ δώσω τοῖς δυσὶν μάρτυσίν μου, καὶ προφητεύσουσιν ἡμέρας χιλίας διακοσίας ἑξήκοντα περιβεβλημένοι σάκκους. 4 οὗτοί εἰσιν αἱ δύο ἐλαῖαι καὶ αἱ δύο λυχνίαι αἱ ἐνώπιον τοῦ κυρίου τῆς γῆς ἑστῶτες· 5 καὶ εἴ τις αὐτοὺς θέλει ἀδικῆσαι, πῦρ ἐκπορεύεται ἐκ τοῦ στόματος αὐτῶν καὶ κατεσθίει τοὺς ἐχθροὺς αὐτῶν· καὶ εἴ τις θελήσῃ αὐτοὺς ἀδικῆσαι, οὕτως δεῖ αὐτὸν ἀποκτανθῆναι. 6 οὗτοι ἔχουσιν ἐξουσίαν κλεῖσαι τὸν οὐρανόν, ἵνα μὴ ὑετὸς βρέχῃ τὰς ἡμέρας τῆς προφητείας αὐτῶν, καὶ ἐξουσίαν ἔχουσιν ἐπὶ τῶν ὑδάτων στρέφειν αὐτὰ εἰς αἷμα καὶ πατάξαι τὴν γῆν ἐν πάσῃ πληγῇ ὁσάκις ἐὰν θελήσωσιν. 7 καὶ ὅταν τελέσωσιν τὴν μαρτυρίαν αὐτῶν, τὸ θηρίον * ποιήσει μετ' αὐτῶν πόλεμον καὶ νικήσει αὐτοὺς καὶ ἀποκτενεῖ αὐτούς. 8 καὶ τὸ πτῶμα αὐτῶν ἐπὶ τῆς πλατείας τῆς πόλεως τῆς μεγάλης, ἥτις καλεῖται πνευματικῶς Σόδομα καὶ Αἴγυπτος, ὅπου καὶ ὁ κύριος αὐτῶν ἐσταυρώθη. 9 καὶ βλέπουσιν ἐκ τῶν λαῶν καὶ φυλῶν καὶ γλωσσῶν καὶ ἐθνῶν τὸ πτῶμα αὐτῶν ἡμέρας τρεῖς καὶ ἥμισυ, καὶ τὰ πτώματα αὐτῶν οὐκ ἀφίουσιν τεθῆναι εἰς μνῆμα. 10 καὶ οἱ κατοικοῦντες ἐπὶ τῆς γῆς χαίρουσιν ἐπ' αὐτοῖς καὶ εὐφραίνονται, καὶ δῶρα πέμπουσιν ἀλλήλοις, ὅτι οὗτοι οἱ δύο προφῆται ἐβασάνισαν τοὺς κατοικοῦντας ἐπὶ τῆς γῆς. 11 καὶ μετὰ τρεῖς ἡμέρας καὶ ἥμισυ πνεῦμα ζωῆς ἐκ τοῦ θεοῦ εἰσῆλθεν ἐν αὐτοῖς, καὶ ἔστησαν ἐπὶ τοὺς πόδας αὐτῶν, καὶ φόβος μέγας ἐπέπεσεν ἐπὶ τοὺς θεωροῦντας αὐτούς. 12 καὶ ἤκουσαν φωνῆς μεγάλης ἐκ τοῦ οὐρανοῦ λεγούσης αὐτοῖς· ἀνάβατε ὧδε· καὶ ἀνέβησαν εἰς τὸν οὐρανὸν ἐν τῇ νεφέλῃ, καὶ ἐθεώρησαν αὐτοὺς οἱ ἐχθροὶ αὐτῶν. 13 καὶ ἐν ἐκείνῃ τῇ ὥρᾳ ἐγένετο σεισμὸς μέγας, καὶ τὸ δέκατον τῆς πόλεως ἔπεσεν, καὶ ἀπεκτάνθησαν ἐν τῷ σεισμῷ ὀνόματα ἀνθρώπων χιλιάδες ἑπτά, καὶ οἱ λοιποὶ ἔμφοβοι ἐγένοντο. καὶ ἔδωκαν δόξαν τῷ Θεῷ τοῦ οὐρανοῦ.

§ VI

Summary to the Story of Prophecy

xi. 1 And a reed, like a measuring rod, was given me, saying: Rise and measure the temple of God, and the altar and the worshippers at it[1]. 2 The court outside the temple omit and measure it not[2], because it has been given over to the nations. And the Holy City they shall tread down forty-two months[3]. 3 Yet I will endow my two witnesses that, clothed in sackcloth[4], they shall prophesy one thousand two hundred and sixty days. 4 These are the two olives with the two lamps which stand before the Lord of the earth[5]. 5 And if any one would wrong them, fire goes out of their mouth and consumes their enemies[6]; yea would any one wrong them, even so must he be slain. 6 These have power to shut up the heavens that rain fall not during the days of their prophesying[7]. And they have power over the waters to turn them into blood; and, as often as they will, to smite the earth with every plague[8]. 7 But, when they shall have completed their witness, the beast shall make war with them and conquer them and slay them. 8 Then their corpse lies on the street of the Great City, which allegorically is named Sodom and Egypt, where also their Lord was crucified. 9 And from peoples, tribes, languages, nations, men look on their corpses three days and a half and do not allow their corpses to be laid in a tomb[9]. 10 And the dwellers on the earth rejoice and exult over them and send presents to each other, because these two prophets tormented those dwelling on the earth. 11 But after three and a half days, a spirit of life from God entered into them, and they stood on their feet. Then great fear fell on those beholding them. 12 And I heard a great voice from heaven saying to them: Come up hither. And they went up to heaven in the cloud, while their enemies beheld them. 13 In that same hour a great earthquake befell; and the tenth of the city fell away, and there were slain in the earthquake seven thousand persons[10], and the rest were terror-stricken: and gave glory to the God of heaven.

[1] Ez. xl. 3 ff. [2] Ez. xlii. 15. Now when he had made an end of measuring the inner house, he brought me forth...and measured it round about. [3] Lk. xxi. 24. And Jerusalem shall be trodden down of the Gentiles, until the times of the Gentiles be fulfilled. Dan. xii. 7. And held up his right hand and his left hand unto heaven and sware by him that liveth forever that it shall be for a time and times and half a time (=3½ years, 42 months, or 1260 days). [4] Is. xx. 2. Loose the sackcloth from thy loins. [5] Zech. iv. 11. Two olive trees upon the right side of the lampstand and on the left thereof. *v.* 14. These are the two sons of oil that stand by the Lord of the whole earth. [6] Jer. v. 14. I will make my words in thy mouth fire, and this people wood, and it shall devour them. [7] 1 K. xvii. 1. There shall not be dew nor rain these years, but according to my word (*i.e.* Elijah's). [8] Ex. vii. 19 ff. (Waters turned into blood and the other plagues of Egypt by Moses.) [9] Dan. ix. 27. And for the half of a week he shall cause the sacrifice and the oblation to cease. [10] Dan. viii. 24. And he shall destroy the mighty ones and the people of the saints.

§ VIII

Ch. xii. 1–14

1 Καὶ σημεῖον μέγα ὤφθη ἐν τῷ οὐρανῷ, γυνὴ περιβεβλημένη τὸν ἥλιον, καὶ ἡ σελήνη ὑποκάτω τῶν ποδῶν αὐτῆς, καὶ ἐπὶ τῆς κεφαλῆς αὐτῆς στέφανος ἀστέρων δώδεκα, 2 καὶ ἐν γαστρὶ ἔχουσα, καὶ κράζει ὠδίνουσα καὶ βασανιζομένη τεκεῖν. 3 καὶ ὤφθη ἄλλο σημεῖον ἐν τῷ οὐρανῷ, καὶ ἰδοὺ δράκων πυρρὸς μέγας, ἔχων κεφαλὰς ἑπτὰ καὶ κέρατα δέκα καὶ ἐπὶ τὰς κεφαλὰς αὐτοῦ ἑπτὰ διαδήματα, 4 καὶ ἡ οὐρὰ αὐτοῦ σύρει τὸ τρίτον τῶν ἀστέρων τοῦ οὐρανοῦ, καὶ ἔβαλεν αὐτοὺς εἰς τὴν γῆν. καὶ ὁ δράκων ἕστηκεν ἐνώπιον τῆς γυναικὸς τῆς μελλούσης τεκεῖν, ἵνα ὅταν τέκῃ τὸ τέκνον αὐτῆς καταφάγῃ. 5 καὶ ἔτεκεν υἱὸν ἄρσεν, ὃς μέλλει ποιμαίνειν πάντα τὰ ἔθνη ἐν ῥάβδῳ σιδηρᾷ· καὶ ἡρπάσθη τὸ τέκνον αὐτῆς πρὸς τὸν θεὸν καὶ πρὸς τὸν θρόνον αὐτοῦ. 6 καὶ ἡ γυνὴ ἔφυγεν εἰς τὴν ἔρημον, ὅπου ἔχει ἐκεῖ τόπον ἡτοιμασμένον ἀπὸ τοῦ θεοῦ, ἵνα ἐκεῖ τρέφουσιν αὐτὴν ἡμέρας χιλίας διακοσίας ἑξήκοντα. 7 καὶ ἐγένετο πόλεμος ἐν τῷ οὐρανῷ, ὁ Μιχαὴλ καὶ οἱ ἄγγελοι αὐτοῦ πολεμῆσαι μετὰ τοῦ δράκοντος. καὶ ὁ δράκων ἐπολέμησεν καὶ οἱ ἄγγελοι αὐτοῦ, 8 καὶ οὐκ ἴσχυσαν, οὐδὲ τόπος εὑρέθη αὐτῶν ἔτι ἐν τῷ οὐρανῷ. 9 καὶ ἐβλήθη ὁ δράκων ὁ μέγας, ὁ ὄφις ὁ ἀρχαῖος, ὁ καλούμενος διάβολος καὶ ὁ σατανᾶς, ὁ πλανῶν τὴν οἰκουμένην ὅλην, ἐβλήθη εἰς τὴν γῆν, καὶ οἱ ἄγγελοι αὐτοῦ μετ' αὐτοῦ ἐβλήθησαν. 10 καὶ ἤκουσα φωνὴν μεγάλην ἐν τῷ οὐρανῷ λέγουσαν· ἄρτι ἐγένετο ἡ σωτηρία καὶ ἡ δύναμις καὶ ἡ βασιλεία τοῦ θεοῦ ἡμῶν καὶ ἡ ἐξουσία τοῦ Χριστοῦ αὐτοῦ, ὅτι ἐβλήθη ὁ κατήγωρ τῶν ἀδελφῶν ἡμῶν, ὁ κατηγορῶν αὐτοὺς ἐνώπιον τοῦ θεοῦ ἡμῶν ἡμέρας καὶ νυκτός. 11 καὶ αὐτοὶ ἐνίκησαν αὐτὸν διὰ τὸ αἷμα τοῦ ἀρνίου καὶ διὰ τὸν λόγον τῆς μαρτυρίας αὐτῶν, καὶ οὐκ ἠγάπησαν τὴν ψυχὴν αὐτῶν ἄχρι θανάτου. 12 διὰ τοῦτο εὐφραίνεσθε, οὐρανοὶ καὶ οἱ ἐν αὐτοῖς σκηνοῦντες· οὐαὶ τὴν γῆν καὶ τὴν θάλασσαν, ὅτι κατέβη ὁ διάβολος πρὸς ὑμᾶς ἔχων θυμὸν μέγαν, εἰδὼς ὅτι ὀλίγον καιρὸν ἔχει. 13 καὶ ὅτε εἶδεν ὁ δράκων ὅτι ἐβλήθη εἰς τὴν γῆν, ἐδίωξεν τὴν γυναῖκα ἥτις ἔτεκεν τὸν ἄρσενα. 14 καὶ ἐδόθησαν τῇ γυναικὶ αἱ δύο πτέρυγες τοῦ ἀετοῦ τοῦ μεγάλου, ἵνα πέτηται εἰς τὴν

§ VIII

Fall of Satanic Powers

xii. 1 A great sign appeared in heaven, a woman clothed with the sun, the moon under her feet and on her head a crown of twelve stars. 2 And she was with child and cried out, being in labour and pain to bring forth[1]. 3 Then another sign appeared in heaven: Lo, a great red dragon having seven heads and ten horns and on his heads seven diadems, 4 and his tail sweeps down a third of the stars of heaven and cast them to earth[2]. And the dragon stood before the woman who was about to bring forth, that when she had brought forth, he might eat up her child. 5 And she brought forth a male child, who is hereafter to shepherd all the nations with an iron rod[3]. And her child was snatched up before God and before His throne. 6 Then the woman fled into the wilderness, where she has a place prepared for her by God that there they may nourish her one thousand two hundred and sixty days. 7 Then there was war in heaven, Michael and his angels at war with the dragon. And the dragon and his angels warred, 8 yet they could not prevail, nor was their place found any more in heaven, 9 but the great dragon, the ancient serpent, he who is called Devil and Satan, the deceiver of the whole civilised world, was cast down. He was cast down to earth and his angels were cast down with him. 10 And I heard a great voice in heaven saying, From henceforth is the salvation and the power and the dominion of our God and the authority of His Christ, because the accuser of our brethren, who accuses them day and night before our God, is cast down[4]; 11 and they have conquered him through the blood of the Lamb and through the word of their witness, and have not loved their lives even to death. 12 Wherefore, rejoice, O heavens, and ye who tabernacle in them. Woe to earth and sea, because the devil has come down to you, having great rage, knowing that he has only a little time. 13 Then, when the dragon saw that he was cast down to earth, he persecuted the woman who bare the male child. 14 And there were given to the woman the two wings of the great eagle that she might flee into the

[1] Mic. iv. 7–9. The Lord shall reign over them in mount Zion...unto thee shall it come; yea the former dominion shall come, the kingdom of the daughter of Jerusalem. Now why dost thou cry out aloud?...that pangs have taken hold of thee as of a woman in travail. Be in pain and labour to bring forth, O daughter of Zion. [2] Dan. viii. 10. And it waxed great even to the hosts of heaven; and some of the host and of the stars it cast down to the ground and trampled upon them, yea, it magnified itself even to the prince of the host...and it took away from him the continual burnt-offering, and the place of his sanctuary was cast down. And it cast down truth to the ground.
[3] Dan. ix. 24. And to bring in everlasting righteousness. Ps. ii. 7–9. Thou art my son, this day have I begotten thee...I will give the nations for thine inheritance.... Thou shalt break them with a rod of iron (used also in Rev. ii. 27 and xix. 15).
[4] Job i. Dan. vii. 7. (Some identification with the fourth beast) and it was diverse from all the beasts that were before it; and it had ten horns.

§ IX

Ch. xii. 14—xiii. 11

ἔρημον εἰς τὸν τόπον αὐτῆς, ὅπου τρέφεται ἐκεῖ καιρὸν καὶ καιροὺς καὶ ἥμισυ καιροῦ ἀπὸ προσώπου τοῦ ὄφεως. 15 καὶ ἔβαλεν ὁ ὄφις ἐκ τοῦ στόματος αὐτοῦ ὀπίσω τῆς γυναικὸς ὕδωρ ὡς ποταμόν, ἵνα αὐτὴν ποταμοφόρητον ποιήσῃ. 16 καὶ ἐβοήθησεν ἡ γῆ τῇ γυναικί, καὶ ἤνοιξεν ἡ γῆ τὸ στόμα αὐτῆς καὶ κατέπιεν τὸν ποταμὸν ὃν ἔβαλεν ὁ δράκων ἐκ τοῦ στόματος αὐτοῦ. 17 καὶ ὠργίσθη ὁ δράκων ἐπὶ τῇ γυναικί, καὶ ἀπῆλθεν ποιῆσαι πόλεμον μετὰ τῶν λοιπῶν τοῦ σπέρματος αὐτῆς τῶν τηρούντων τὰς ἐντολὰς τοῦ θεοῦ καὶ ἐχόντων τὴν μαρτυρίαν Ἰησοῦ. 18 καὶ ἐστάθην ἐπὶ τὴν ἄμμον τῆς θαλάσσης. 1 καὶ εἶδον ἐκ τῆς θαλάσσης θηρίον ἀναβαῖνον, ἔχον κέρατα δέκα καὶ κεφαλὰς ἑπτά, καὶ ἐπὶ τῶν κεράτων αὐτοῦ δέκα διαδήματα, καὶ ἐπὶ τὰς κεφαλὰς αὐτοῦ ὀνόματα βλασφημίας. 2 καὶ τὸ θηρίον ὃ εἶδον ἦν ὅμοιον παρδάλει, καὶ οἱ πόδες αὐτοῦ ὡς ἄρκου, καὶ τὸ στόμα αὐτοῦ ὡς στόμα λεόντων· καὶ ἔδωκεν αὐτῷ ὁ δράκων τὴν δύναμιν αὐτοῦ καὶ τὸν θρόνον αὐτοῦ καὶ ἐξουσίαν μεγάλην. 3 καὶ μίαν ἐκ τῶν κεφαλῶν αὐτοῦ ὡς ἐσφαγμένην εἰς θάνατον, καὶ ἡ πληγὴ τοῦ θανάτου αὐτοῦ ἐθεραπεύθη. καὶ ἐθαύμασεν ὅλη ἡ γῆ ὀπίσω τοῦ θηρίου, 4 καὶ προσεκύνησαν τῷ δράκοντι, ὅτι ἔδωκεν τὴν ἐξουσίαν τῷ θηρίῳ, καὶ προσεκύνησαν τῷ θηρίῳ λέγοντες· τίς ὅμοιος τῷ θηρίῳ, καὶ τίς δύναται πολεμῆσαι μετ᾽ αὐτοῦ; 5 καὶ ἐδόθη αὐτῷ στόμα λαλοῦν μεγάλα καὶ βλασφημίας, καὶ ἐδόθη αὐτῷ ἐξουσία ποιῆσαι μῆνας τεσσεράκοντα δύο. 6 καὶ ἤνοιξεν τὸ στόμα αὐτοῦ εἰς βλασφημίας πρὸς τὸν θεόν, βλασφημῆσαι τὸ ὄνομα αὐτοῦ καὶ τὴν σκηνὴν αὐτοῦ, τοὺς ἐν τῷ οὐρανῷ σκηνοῦντας. 7 καὶ ἐδόθη αὐτῷ ποιῆσαι πόλεμον μετὰ τῶν ἁγίων καὶ νικῆσαι αὐτούς, καὶ ἐδόθη αὐτῷ ἐξουσία ἐπὶ πᾶσαν φυλὴν καὶ λαὸν καὶ γλῶσσαν καὶ ἔθνος. 8 καὶ προσκυνήσουσιν αὐτὸν πάντες οἱ κατοικοῦντες ἐπὶ τῆς γῆς, οὗ οὐ γέγραπται τὸ ὄνομα αὐτοῦ ἐν τῷ βιβλίῳ τῆς ζωῆς τοῦ ἀρνίου τοῦ ἐσφαγμένου ἀπὸ καταβολῆς κόσμου. * 10 εἴ τις εἰς αἰχμαλωσίαν, εἰς αἰχμαλωσίαν ὑπάγει· εἴ τις ἐν μαχαίρῃ ἀποκτενεῖ, δεῖ αὐτὸν ἐν μαχαίρῃ ἀποκτανθῆναι. ὧδέ ἐστιν ἡ ὑπομονὴ καὶ ἡ πίστις τῶν ἁγίων. 11 καὶ εἶδον ἄλλο θηρίον ἀναβαῖνον ἐκ τῆς

§ IX

Origin of the World-Kingdoms

xii. 14 wilderness, into her place, where she is sustained a time and times and half a time out of sight of the serpent. 15 And the serpent cast from his mouth after the woman water like a river[1], that it might carry her away in flood. 16 But the earth helped the woman, for the earth opened its mouth and swallowed the river which the dragon cast out of his mouth. 17 Then the dragon was enraged at the woman and went away to make war against the rest of her seed, even those who hold fast the commandments of God and have the witness of Jesus. 18 Then I stood on the shore of the sea, xiii. 1 and I saw rising out of the sea a beast having ten horns and seven heads, and on its horns ten diadems and on its heads names of blasphemy. 2 The beast which I saw was like a leopard, with his feet as a bear's and his mouth as the mouth of lions. To him the dragon gave his power and his throne and great authority[2]. 3 When one of his heads was as smitten unto death, then the stroke of his death was healed. And all the earth marvelled following the beast, 4 and they worshipped the dragon, because he gave authority to the beast; and they worshipped the beast, saying: Who is like the beast and who is able to war with him? 5 There was given to him a mouth speaking arrogancies and blasphemies[3], and there was given him authority to act during forty-two months. 6 And he opened his mouth in blasphemies against God, to blaspheme His name and His dwelling-place, even those dwelling in heaven. 7 And it was given him to make war with the saints and to vanquish them; and authority was given him over every tribe and people and language and nation. 8 And all dwelling on the earth shall worship him, each one whose name is not written, from the foundation of the world, in the roll of life of the Lamb who was slain. 10 If anyone brings into captivity, he goes into captivity; if any slay with the sword, he must be slain by the sword[4]. Herein is the patience and the faith of the saints. 11 And I saw another beast coming up out of

[1] Is. lix. 7. They belch out with their mouth.... *v.* 12. For cursing and lying which they speak. [2] Dan. vii. 4–8. And four great beasts came up from the sea...the first was like a lion...a second like to a bear...and lo another like a leopard...the beast also had four heads: and dominion was given to it...and behold a fourth beast, terrible and powerful, and strong exceedingly. [3] Dan. vii. 8. And a mouth speaking great things. *v.* 25. And he shall speak words against the Most High, and shall wear out the saints of the Most High: and he shall think to change the times and the law; and they shall be given into his hands until a time and times and half a time. [4] Ps. lxviii. 18. Read as Eph. iv. 8. He leadeth captivity captive. Mt. xxvi. 52. For all they that take the sword shall perish with the sword.

§ X

Ch. xiii. 11—18, xiv. 6–12

γῆς, καὶ εἶχεν κέρατα δύο ὅμοια ἀρνίῳ καὶ ἐλάλει ὡς δράκων. 12 καὶ τὴν ἐξουσίαν τοῦ πρώτου θηρίου πᾶσαν ποιεῖ ἐνώπιον αὐτοῦ. καὶ ποιεῖ τὴν γῆν καὶ τοὺς ἐν αὐτῇ κατοικοῦντας ἵνα προσκυνήσουσιν τὸ θηρίον τὸ πρῶτον, οὗ ἐθεραπεύθη ἡ πληγὴ τοῦ θανάτου αὐτοῦ. 13 καὶ ποιεῖ σημεῖα μεγάλα, ἵνα καὶ πῦρ ποιῇ καταβαίνειν ἐκ τοῦ οὐρανοῦ εἰς τὴν γῆν ἐνώπιον τῶν ἀνθρώπων. 14 καὶ πλανᾷ τοὺς κατοικοῦντας ἐπὶ τῆς γῆς διὰ τὰ σημεῖα ἃ ἐδόθη αὐτῷ ποιῆσαι ἐνώπιον τοῦ θηρίου, λέγων τοῖς κατοικοῦσιν ἐπὶ τῆς γῆς ποιῆσαι εἰκόνα τῷ θηρίῳ, ὃς ἔχει τὴν πληγὴν τῆς μαχαίρης καὶ ἔζησεν. 15 καὶ ἐδόθη αὐτῷ δοῦναι πνεῦμα τῇ εἰκόνι τοῦ θηρίου, ἵνα καὶ λαλήσῃ ἡ εἰκὼν τοῦ θηρίου, καὶ ποιήσῃ ὅσοι ἐὰν μὴ προσκυνήσουσιν τῇ εἰκόνι τοῦ θηρίου ἀποκτανθῶσιν. 16 καὶ ποιεῖ πάντας, τοὺς μικροὺς καὶ τοὺς μεγάλους, καὶ τοὺς πλουσίους καὶ τοὺς πτωχούς, καὶ τοὺς ἐλευθέρους καὶ τοὺς δούλους, ἵνα δῶσιν αὐτοῖς χάραγμα ἐπὶ τῆς χειρὸς αὐτῶν τῆς δεξιᾶς ἢ ἐπὶ τὸ μέτωπον αὐτῶν, 17 ἵνα μή τις δύνηται ἀγοράσαι ἢ πωλῆσαι εἰ μὴ ὁ ἔχων τὸ χάραγμα τὸ ὄνομα τοῦ θηρίου ἢ τὸν ἀριθμὸν τοῦ ὀνόματος αὐτοῦ. 18 ὧδε ἡ σοφία ἐστίν. ὁ ἔχων νοῦν ψηφισάτω τὸν ἀριθμὸν τοῦ θηρίου· ἀριθμὸς γὰρ ἀνθρώπου ἐστίν. καὶ ὁ ἀριθμὸς αὐτοῦ χξσ′[1]. * 6 Καὶ εἶδον ἄλλον ἄγγελον πετόμενον ἐν μεσουρανήματι, ἔχοντα εὐαγγέλιον αἰώνιον εὐαγγελίσαι ἐπὶ τοὺς καθημένους ἐπὶ τῆς γῆς καὶ ἐπὶ πᾶν ἔθνος καὶ φυλὴν καὶ γλῶσσαν καὶ λαόν, 7 λέγων ἐν φωνῇ μεγάλῃ· φοβήθητε τὸν θεὸν καὶ δότε αὐτῷ δόξαν, ὅτι ἦλθεν ἡ ὥρα τῆς κρίσεως αὐτοῦ, καὶ προσκυνήσατε τῷ ποιήσαντι τὸν οὐρανὸν καὶ τὴν γῆν καὶ τὴν θάλασσαν καὶ πηγὰς ὑδάτων. * 9 Καὶ ἄλλος ἄγγελος τρίτος ἠκολούθησεν αὐτοῖς λέγων ἐν φωνῇ μεγάλῃ· εἴ τις προσκυνεῖ τὸ θηρίον καὶ τὴν εἰκόνα αὐτοῦ, καὶ λαμβάνει χάραγμα ἐπὶ τοῦ μετώπου αὐτοῦ ἢ ἐπὶ τὴν χεῖρα αὐτοῦ, 10 καὶ αὐτὸς πίεται ἐκ τοῦ οἴνου τοῦ θυμοῦ τοῦ θεοῦ τοῦ κεκερασμένου ἀκράτου ἐν τῷ ποτηρίῳ τῆς ὀργῆς αὐτοῦ, καὶ βασανισθήσεται ἐν πυρὶ καὶ θείῳ ἐνώπιον ἀγγέλων ἁγίων καὶ ἐνώπιον τοῦ ἀρνίου. * 12 ὧδε ἡ ὑπομονὴ τῶν ἁγίων ἐστίν, οἱ τηροῦντες τὰς ἐντολὰς τοῦ θεοῦ καὶ τὴν πίστιν Ἰησοῦ.

[1] Text ϛ.

§ X

The False Prophet and the True

xiii. 11 the earth, and he had two horns like a lamb[1], but he spoke like a dragon. 12 All the authority of the first beast he exercises before him. And he works on the earth and those dwelling on it that they should worship the first beast the stroke of whose death was healed. 13 He does great signs, even to making fire come down from heaven to earth in the sight of men. 14 And he deceives the dwellers on the earth through the signs which were given him to do before the beast, telling those who dwell on the earth to make an image to the beast which has the stroke of the sword, and came to life. 15 And it was given to him to give a spirit to the image of the beast, so that the image of the beast might speak and might cause as many as would not worship the image of the beast to be put to death. 16 And he causes all —small and great, rich and poor, freemen and slaves—that he may give them a mark on their right hand or on their forehead, 17 that no one be able to buy or sell unless he have the mark, the name of the beast or the number of his name. 18 Herein is wisdom. Let him who has understanding count up the number of the beast, for it is a number of a man; and the number of it is 1000 + 60 + 200[2]. xiv. 6 Then I saw another angel flying in mid-heaven, one having an eternal gospel, to give good news to the inhabitants of the earth, even every nation, tribe, language, people. 7 With a great voice he is saying: Fear God and give Him glory, for the hour of His judgment has come. Worship the maker of the heaven and the earth and the sea and fountains of waters. 9 And another, a third angel, followed them saying with a great voice: If anyone worship the beast and his image and receive a mark on his forehead or on his hand, 10 he also shall drink of the wine of God's anger, mixed unwatered in the cup of His wrath[3], and he will be tried in fire and brimstone before holy angels and before the Lamb. 12 Herein is the patience of the saints who hold fast the commandments of God and the faith of Jesus.

[1] Dan. viii. 3. A ram which had two horns. [2] Dan. xii. 7–10. It shall be for a time, times and a half....And I heard, but I understood not...but the wicked shall do wickedly; and none of the wicked shall understand, but they that be wise shall understand. [3] Is. li. 17. Which hast drunk at the hand of the Lord the cup of his fury.

§ XI

Ch. xv. 5–6, xvi. 2–16 and viii. 6–11[1]

5 Καὶ μετὰ ταῦτα ἴδον, καὶ ἠνοίγη ὁ ναὸς τῆς σκηνῆς τοῦ μαρτυρίου ἐν τῷ οὐρανῷ, 6 καὶ ἐξῆλθον οἱ ἑπτὰ ἄγγελοι οἱ ἔχοντες τὰς ἑπτὰ πληγὰς ἐκ τοῦ ναοῦ, ἐνδεδυμένοι λίνον καθαρὸν λαμπρόν. 2 καὶ ἀπῆλθεν ὁ πρῶτος καὶ ἐξέχεεν τὴν φιάλην αὐτοῦ εἰς τὴν γῆν· (καὶ ἐγένετο χάλαζα καὶ πῦρ μεμιγμένον ἐν αἵματι καὶ τὸ τρίτον τῶν δένδρων καὶ πᾶς χόρτος χλωρὸς κατεκάη.) καὶ ἐγένετο ἕλκος κακὸν καὶ πονηρὸν ἐπὶ τοὺς ἀνθρώπους. * 3 καὶ ὁ δεύτερος ἐξέχεεν τὴν φιάλην αὐτοῦ εἰς τὴν θάλασσαν· (ὡς ὄρος μέγα πυρὶ καιόμενον.) καὶ πᾶσα ψυχὴ ζωῆς ἀπέθανεν, τὰ ἐν τῇ θαλάσσῃ. καὶ ἐγένετο ὡς νεκροῦ. * 4 καὶ ὁ τρίτος ἐξέχεεν τὴν φιάλην αὐτοῦ εἰς τοὺς ποταμοὺς καὶ τὰς πηγὰς τῶν ὑδάτων. (καὶ ἔπεσεν ἐκ τοῦ οὐρανοῦ ἀστὴρ μέγας καιόμενος ὡς λαμπάς. 11 καὶ τὸ ὄνομα τοῦ ἀστέρος λέγεται ὁ ἄψινθος. καὶ ἐγένετο τὸ τρίτον τῶν ὑδάτων εἰς ἄψινθον, καὶ πολλοὶ τῶν ἀνθρώπων ἀπέθανον ἐκ τῶν ὑδάτων ὅτι ἐπικράνθησαν.) 8 καὶ ὁ τέταρτος ἐξέχεεν τὴν φιάλην αὐτοῦ ἐπὶ τὸν ἥλιον, καὶ ἐδόθη αὐτῷ καυματίσαι τοὺς ἀνθρώπους ἐν πυρί. 9 καὶ ἐκαυματίσθησαν οἱ ἄνθρωποι καῦμα μέγα, καὶ ἐβλασφήμησαν τὸ ὄνομα θεοῦ ἐπὶ τὰς πληγὰς ταύτας, καὶ οὐ μετενόησαν δοῦναι αὐτῷ δόξαν. 10 καὶ ὁ πέμπτος ἐξέχεεν τὴν φιάλην αὐτοῦ ἐπὶ τὸν θρόνον τοῦ θηρίου· καὶ ἐγένετο ἡ βασιλεία αὐτοῦ ἐσκοτωμένη, καὶ ἐμασῶντο τὰς γλώσσας αὐτῶν ἐκ τοῦ πόνου. 11 καὶ ἐβλασφήμησαν τὸν θεὸν τοῦ οὐρανοῦ ἐκ τῶν πόνων αὐτῶν καὶ ἐκ τῶν ἑλκῶν αὐτῶν, καὶ οὐ μετενόησαν ἐκ τῶν ἔργων αὐτῶν. 12 καὶ ὁ ἕκτος ἐξέχεεν τὴν φιάλην αὐτοῦ ἐπὶ τὸν ποταμὸν * τὸν Εὐφράτην· καὶ ἐξηράνθη τὸ ὕδωρ αὐτοῦ, ἵνα ἑτοιμασθῇ ἡ ὁδὸς τῶν βασιλέων τῶν ἀπὸ ἀνατολῆς ἡλίου. 13 καὶ ἴδον ἐκ τοῦ στόματος τοῦ δράκοντος καὶ ἐκ τοῦ στόματος τοῦ θηρίου καὶ ἐκ τοῦ στόματος τοῦ ψευδοπροφήτου πνεύματα τρία ἀκάθαρτα ὡς βάτραχοι· 14 εἰσὶν γὰρ πνεύματα δαιμονίων ποιοῦντα σημεῖα, ἃ ἐκπορεύεται ἐπὶ τοὺς βασιλεῖς τῆς οἰκουμένης ὅλης, συναγαγεῖν αὐτοὺς εἰς τὸν πόλεμον τῆς ἡμέρας τῆς μεγάλης τοῦ θεοῦ τοῦ παντοκράτορος. * 16 καὶ συνήγαγεν αὐτοὺς εἰς τὸν τόπον τὸν καλούμενον Ἑβραϊστὶ Ἁρμαγεδών.

[1] Passages in brackets from ch. viii.

§ XI

THE FIRST SIX MONARCHIES

xv. 5 Thereupon I saw that the temple of the tent of witness in heaven was opened: 6 and from the temple came out the seven angels having the seven plagues, clothed in linen pure and bright. xvi. 2 And the first went and poured his vial on the land (and it was hail and fire mingled with blood[1], and a third of the trees and all green grass was burned up[2]) and it became a sore, foul and evil upon men[3]. 3 And the third poured out his vial on the sea (as a great mountain burning with fire[4]). And every living creature died that was in the sea; and it was as a sea of the dead. 4 And the third poured out his vial on the rivers and fountains of waters; (and it fell from heaven a great star blazing like a torch[5]. 11 And the name of the star is called Wormwood[6]. And a third of the water became wormwood, and many of the men died of the waters, because they were embittered)[7]. 8 And the fourth poured his vial on the sun: and it was given to him to burn men with fire. 9 And men were burned a great burning[8]: and blasphemed the name of God, for these plagues, and did not repent to give him glory. 10 And the fifth poured out his vial on the throne of the beast: and his kingdom was darkened. And they gnawed their tongues for the pain. 11 And they blasphemed the God of heaven for their pains and their sores, and did not repent of their works. 12 Then the sixth angel poured out his vial on the river, the Euphrates. And the water of it was dried up that the way of the kings of the East might be made ready. 13 Then I saw from the mouth of the dragon and from the mouth of the beast and from the mouth of the false prophet three unclean spirits like frogs, 14 which are spirits of demons working miracles, which go out to the kings of the whole civilised world to gather them unto the battle of the great day of the all-sovereign God[9], 16 and they gathered them to the place which is called in Hebrew Har-magedon[10].

[1] Ex. ix. 24. Hail and fire mingled with hail. [2] Ex. ix. 25. It smote every herb and brake every tree. [3] Ex. ix. 9. A boil breaking forth with blains. [4] Deut. iv. 11. A mountain burning to the heart of heaven. [5] Is. xiv. 12. How art thou fallen from heaven, O Day Star. [6] Jer. ix. 15. I will feed them with wormwood, and give them the water of gall to drink. [7] Pro. x. 4. Her end is bitter as wormwood. [8] Is. x. 16. Under his glory there shall be kindled a burning like the burning of fire—(of Assyria). [9] 1 K. xxii. 23. I will go forth and will be a lying spirit in the mouth of all his prophets...thou shalt entice him. [10] Dan. xi. 45. And he shall plant the tents of his palace between the sea and the glorious holy mountain; yet he shall come to an end and none shall help him.

§ XII

Ch. xix. 11–15, xiv. 19–20, xix. 16–21

11 καὶ εἶδον τὸν οὐρανὸν ἠνεῳγμένον, καὶ ἰδοὺ ἵππος λευκός, καὶ ὁ καθήμενος ἐπ' αὐτὸν καλούμενος πιστὸς καὶ ἀληθινός, καὶ ἐν δικαιοσύνῃ κρίνει καὶ πολεμεῖ. 12 οἱ δὲ ὀφθαλμοὶ αὐτοῦ φλὸξ πυρός, καὶ ἐπὶ τὴν κεφαλὴν αὐτοῦ διαδήματα πολλά, ἔχων ὄνομα γεγραμμένον ὃ οὐδεὶς οἶδεν εἰ μὴ αὐτός, 13 καὶ περιβεβλημένος ἱμάτιον περιρεραμμένον αἵματι, καὶ κέκληται τὸ ὄνομα αὐτοῦ ὁ λόγος τοῦ θεοῦ. 14 καὶ τὰ στρατεύματα ἐν τῷ οὐρανῷ ἠκολούθει αὐτῷ ἐφ' ἵπποις λευκοῖς, ἐνδεδυμένοι βύσσινον λευκὸν καθαρόν. 15 καὶ ἐκ τοῦ στόματος αὐτοῦ ἐκπορεύεται ῥομφαία ὀξεῖα, ἵνα ἐν αὐτῇ πατάξῃ τὰ ἔθνη· καὶ αὐτὸς ποιμανεῖ αὐτοὺς ἐν ῥάβδῳ σιδηρᾷ, καὶ αὐτὸς πατεῖ τὴν ληνὸν τοῦ οἴνου τοῦ θυμοῦ τῆς ὀργῆς τοῦ θεοῦ τοῦ παντοκράτορος. 19 καὶ ἐτρύγησεν καὶ ἔβαλεν εἰς τὴν ληνὸν τοῦ θυμοῦ τοῦ θεοῦ τὸν μέγαν. 20 καὶ ἐπατήθη ἡ ληνὸς ἔξωθεν τῆς πόλεως, καὶ ἐξῆλθεν αἷμα ἐκ τῆς ληνοῦ ἄχρι τῶν χαλινῶν τῶν ἵππων, ἀπὸ σταδίων χιλίων ἑξακοσίων. 16 καὶ ἔχει ἐπὶ τὸ ἱμάτιον καὶ ἐπὶ τὸν μηρὸν αὐτοῦ ὄνομα γεγραμμένον· βασιλεὺς βασιλέων καὶ κύριος κυρίων. 17 καὶ εἶδον ἕνα ἄγγελον ἑστῶτα ἐν τῷ ἡλίῳ, καὶ ἔκραξεν ἐν φωνῇ μεγάλῃ λέγων πᾶσιν τοῖς ὀρνέοις τοῖς πετομένοις ἐν μεσουρανήματι· δεῦτε συνάχθητε εἰς τὸ δεῖπνον τὸ μέγα τοῦ θεοῦ, 18 ἵνα φάγητε σάρκας βασιλέων καὶ σάρκας χιλιάρχων καὶ σάρκας ἰσχυρῶν καὶ σάρκας ἵππων καὶ τῶν καθημένων ἐπ' αὐτῶν, καὶ σάρκας πάντων ἐλευθέρων τε καὶ δούλων καὶ μικρῶν καὶ μεγάλων. 19 καὶ ἴδον τὸ θηρίον καὶ τοὺς βασιλεῖς τῆς γῆς καὶ τὰ στρατεύματα αὐτῶν συνηγμένα ποιῆσαι τὸν πόλεμον μετὰ τοῦ καθημένου ἐπὶ τοῦ ἵππου καὶ μετὰ τοῦ στρατεύματος αὐτοῦ. 20 καὶ ἐπιάσθη τὸ θηρίον καὶ μετ' αὐτοῦ ὁ ψευδοπροφήτης ὁ ποιήσας τὰ σημεῖα ἐνώπιον αὐτοῦ, ἐν οἷς ἐπλάνησεν τοὺς λαβόντας τὸ χάραγμα τοῦ θηρίου καὶ τοὺς προσκυνοῦντας τῇ εἰκόνι αὐτοῦ· ζῶντες ἐβλήθησαν οἱ δύο εἰς τὴν λίμνην τοῦ πυρὸς τῆς καιομένης ἐν θείῳ. 21 καὶ οἱ λοιποὶ ἀπεκτάνθησαν ἐν τῇ ῥομφαίᾳ τοῦ καθημένου ἐπὶ τοῦ ἵππου τῇ ἐξελθούσῃ ἐκ τοῦ στόματος αὐτοῦ, καὶ πάντα τὰ ὄρνεα ἐχορτάσθησαν ἐκ τῶν σαρκῶν αὐτῶν.

§ XII

xix. 11 Then I saw the heaven opened, and lo, a white horse. His rider, called Faithful and True, judges and wars in righteousness[1], 12 his eyes a flame of fire and on his head many diadems, having a name written which no one knows except himself, 13 and clothed in a garment dripping with blood. And his name is called The Word of God. 14 The armies which are in heaven followed him on white horses, clothed in fine linen white and pure. 15 From his mouth goes out a sharp sword that with it he should smite the nations, and it is he who will shepherd them with an iron rod. He too treads the wine-press of the wine of the anger of the wrath of God, the All-sovereign. xiv. 19 And he gathered and cast into the great wine-press of the anger of God; 20 and the wine-press was trodden without the city, and from the wine-press blood went out, up to the bridles of the horses, for one thousand six hundred stadia[2]. xix. 16 On his garment and on his thigh he has a name inscribed, King of kings and Lord of lords. 17 Then I saw an angel standing in the sun, and he cried with a great voice, calling to all the birds that fly in the mid-heaven: Come and be gathered together to God's great supper, 18 that ye may eat the flesh of kings and the flesh of captains and the flesh of mighty men and the flesh of horses and their riders and the flesh of all—freemen and slaves, small and great[3]. 19 Then I saw the beast and the kings of the earth and their armies gathered to make war with the rider on the horse and with his army. 20 Then was mastered the beast and with him the false prophet, the worker of miracles before him, with which he deceived those who received the mark of the beast and worshipped his image. Alive the two were cast into the lake of fire, the lake burning with brimstone[4]. 21 The rest were slain with the sword of him who sits on the horse—the sword which comes out of his mouth; and all the birds were gorged with their flesh[5].

[1] Is. xi. 4, 5. And he shall smite the earth with the rod of his mouth, and with the breath of his lips shall he slay the wicked. And righteousness shall be the girdle of his loins and faithfulness the girdle of his reins. [2] Is. lxiii. 3–6. I trod the wine-press alone,...their life-blood is sprinkled upon my garments, and I have stained all my raiment. For the day of vengeance was in my heart, and the year of my redeemed is come....I poured out their life-blood on the earth. [3] Lk. xvii. 37. Where the body is, thither will the vultures be gathered together. [4] Dan. vii. 11. I beheld even till the beast was slain, and his body destroyed, and he was given to be burned with fire. [5] Ez. xxxix. 4. Thou shalt fall upon the mountains of Israel, thou, and all thy hordes, and of the peoples that are with thee: I will give thee unto the ravenous birds of every sort, and to the beasts of the field to be devoured.

§ XIII

Ch. xvi. 17—xvii. 9

17 Καὶ ὁ ἕβδομος ἐξέχεεν τὴν φιάλην αὐτοῦ ἐπὶ τὸν ἀέρα· καὶ ἐξῆλθεν φωνὴ μεγάλη ἐκ τοῦ ναοῦ ἀπὸ τοῦ θρόνου λέγουσα· γέγονεν. 18 καὶ ἐγένοντο ἀστραπαὶ καὶ φωναὶ καὶ βρονταί. καὶ σεισμὸς ἐγένετο μέγας, οἷος οὐκ ἐγένετο ἀφ' οὗ ἄνθρωπος ἐγένετο ἐπὶ τῆς γῆς, τηλικοῦτος σεισμὸς οὕτω μέγας. 19 καὶ ἐγένετο ἡ πόλις * εἰς τρία[1] μέρη, καὶ αἱ πόλεις τῶν ἐθνῶν ἔπεσαν. καὶ Βαβυλὼν ἡ μεγάλη ἐμνήσθη ἐνώπιον τοῦ θεοῦ δοῦναι αὐτῇ τὸ ποτήριον τοῦ οἴνου τοῦ θυμοῦ τῆς ὀργῆς αὐτοῦ. 20 καὶ πᾶσα νῆσος ἔφυγεν, καὶ ὄρη οὐχ εὑρέθησαν. 21 καὶ χάλαζα μεγάλη ὡς ταλαντιαία καταβαίνει ἐκ τοῦ οὐρανοῦ ἐπὶ τοὺς ἀνθρώπους· * ὅτι μεγάλη ἐστὶν ἡ πληγὴ αὐτῆς σφόδρα. 1 καὶ ἦλθεν εἷς ἐκ τῶν ἑπτὰ ἀγγέλων τῶν ἐχόντων τὰς ἑπτὰ φιάλας, καὶ ἐλάλησεν μετ' ἐμοῦ λέγων· δεῦρο, δείξω σοι τὸ κρίμα τῆς πόρνης τῆς μεγάλης τῆς καθημένης ἐπὶ ὑδάτων πολλῶν, 2 μεθ' ἧς ἐπόρνευσαν οἱ βασιλεῖς τῆς γῆς, καὶ ἐμεθύσθησαν οἱ κατοικοῦντες τὴν γῆν ἐκ τοῦ οἴνου τῆς πορνείας αὐτῆς. 3 καὶ ἀπήνεγκέν με εἰς ἔρημον ἐν πνεύματι. καὶ εἶδον γυναῖκα καθημένην ἐπὶ θηρίον κόκκινον, γέμοντα ὀνόματα βλασφημίας, ἔχοντα κεφαλὰς ἑπτὰ καὶ κέρατα δέκα. 4 καὶ ἡ γυνὴ ἦν περιβεβλημένη πορφυροῦν καὶ κόκκινον, καὶ κεχρυσωμένη χρυσῷ καὶ λίθῳ τιμίῳ καὶ μαργαρίταις, ἔχουσα ποτήριον χρυσοῦν ἐν τῇ χειρὶ αὐτῆς γέμων βδελυγμάτων καὶ τὰ ἀκάθαρτα τῆς πορνείας αὐτῆς, 5 καὶ ἐπὶ τὸ μέτωπον αὐτῆς ὄνομα γεγραμμένον· μυστήριον, Βαβυλὼν ἡ μεγάλη, ἡ μήτηρ τῶν πορνῶν καὶ τῶν βδελυγμάτων τῆς γῆς. 6 καὶ εἶδα τὴν γυναῖκα μεθύουσαν ἐκ τοῦ αἵματος τῶν ἁγίων καὶ ἐκ τοῦ αἵματος τῶν μαρτύρων Ἰησοῦ, καὶ ἐθαύμασα ἰδὼν αὐτὴν θαῦμα μέγα. 7 καὶ εἶπέν μοι ὁ ἄγγελος· διατί ἐθαύμασας; ἐγώ σοι ἐρῶ τὸ μυστήριον τῆς γυναικὸς καὶ τοῦ θηρίου τοῦ βαστάζοντος αὐτὴν τοῦ ἔχοντος τὰς ἑπτὰ κεφαλὰς καὶ τὰ δέκα κέρατα. 8 τὸ θηρίον ὃ εἶδες ἦν καὶ οὐκ ἔστιν, καὶ μέλλει ἀναβαίνειν ἐκ τῆς ἀβύσσου καὶ εἰς ἀπώλειαν ὑπάγειν· καὶ θαυμάσονται οἱ κατοικοῦντες ἐπὶ τῆς γῆς, ὧν οὐ γέγραπται τὸ ὄνομα ἐπὶ τὸ βιβλίον τῆς ζωῆς ἀπὸ καταβολῆς κόσμου, βλεπόντων τὸ θηρίον ὅτι ἦν καὶ οὐκ ἔστιν καὶ παρέσται. 9 ὧδε ὁ νοῦς ὁ

[1] δέκα v. 12.

§ XIII

End of the World-rule

xvi. 17 Then the seventh poured out his vial on the air, and there went forth a great voice out of the temple, from the throne, saying: It is done. 18 And there were lightnings, and voices, and thunders. Then was there a great earthquake: so great an earthquake never was since man was on the earth[1]; 19 and the city parted into three[2], and the cities of the nations fell away. So Babylon the Great was remembered before God, to give her the cup of the wine of the anger of His wrath. 20 Every island fled and hills were not found[3]. 21 And great hail, about a talent weight, comes down from heaven upon men; for the plague of it is great exceedingly. xvii. 1 Then came one of the seven angels who had the seven vials and spake with me saying: Come, I will show thee the judgment of the great harlot, who sits on many waters, 2 with whom the kings of the earth have committed fornication, while the inhabitants of the earth have been made drunk by the wine of her fornication. 3 Then he carried me in spirit into the wilderness, and I saw a woman sitting on a scarlet beast full of names of blasphemy and having seven heads and ten horns[4]. 4 The woman was clothed in purple and scarlet, decked with gold and precious stone and pearls, holding a golden cup in her hand full of abominations—the unclean things of her fornication. 5 On her forehead was a name inscribed, a mystery: 'Babylon the Great, the mother of harlots and of earth's abominations.' 6 I saw that the woman was drunk from the blood of the saints and the blood of the witnesses of Jesus; and seeing her I was amazed with a great amazement. 7 But the angel said to me: Why art thou amazed? I will tell thee the mystery of the woman and of the beast, having the seven heads and ten horns, that carries her. 8 The beast which thou sawest, was and is not, yet is about to come up out of the abyss and to go into destruction[5]. Then the inhabitants of the earth—each one whose name has not been written from the foundation of the world in the book of life—shall be amazed seeing the beast 9 that was and is not, yet is to be. Here understanding *is needed*, whosoever has wisdom![6]

[1] Dan. xii. 1. And there shall be a time of trouble, such as never was since there was a nation even to that time. [2] Dan. vii. 8. Another horn, a little one, before which three of the first horns were plucked up by the roots. [3] Is. ii. 12, 14. A day of the lord of Hosts...upon the hills that are lifted up. [4] Lk. iv. 1–5. And was led by the Spirit into the wilderness...and he showed him all the kingdoms of the world. [5] Dan. viii. 24. And he shall destroy wonderfully. ix. 27. One that maketh desolate. [6] Dan. xii. 10. They that be wise shall understand.

§ XIV

Ch. xvii. 9—xviii. 6

ἔχων σοφίαν. αἱ ἑπτὰ κεφαλαὶ ἑπτὰ ὕδατα εἰσίν, ὅπου ἡ γυνὴ κάθηται ἐπ᾽ αὐτῶν, 10 *καὶ βασιλεῖς ἑπτά εἰσιν· οἱ πέντε ἔπεσαν, ὁ εἷς ἔστιν, ὁ ἄλλος οὔπω ἦλθεν, καὶ ὅταν ἔλθῃ ὀλίγον αὐτὸν δεῖ μεῖναι.* 11 *καὶ τὸ θηρίον ὃ ἦν καὶ οὐκ ἔστιν, καὶ αὐτὸς ὄγδοός ἐστιν, καὶ ἐκ τῶν ἑπτά ἐστιν.* * 12 *καὶ τὰ δέκα κέρατα ἃ εἶδες δέκα βασιλεῖς εἰσίν, οἵτινες βασιλείαν οὔπω ἔλαβον, ἀλλὰ ἐξουσίαν ὡς βασιλεῖς μίαν ὥραν λαμβάνουσιν μετὰ τοῦ θηρίου.* 13 *οὗτοι μίαν γνώμην ἔχουσιν, καὶ τὴν δύναμιν καὶ τὴν ἐξουσίαν αὐτῶν τῷ θηρίῳ διδόασιν.* 14 *οὗτοι μετὰ τοῦ ἀρνίου πολεμήσουσιν καὶ τὸ ἀρνίον νικήσει αὐτούς, ὅτι κύριος κυρίων ἐστὶν καὶ βασιλεὺς βασιλέων. καὶ οἱ μετ᾽ αὐτοῦ κλητοὶ καὶ ἐκλεκτοὶ καὶ πιστοί.* 15 *καὶ λέγει μοι· τὰ ὕδατα ἃ εἶδες, οὗ ἡ πόρνη κάθηται, λαοὶ καὶ ὄχλοι εἰσὶν καὶ ἔθνη καὶ γλῶσσαι.* 16 *καὶ τὰ δέκα κέρατα ἃ εἶδες καὶ τὸ θηρίον, οὗτοι μισήσουσιν τὴν πόρνην, καὶ ἠρημωμένην ποιήσουσιν αὐτὴν καὶ γυμνήν, καὶ τὰς σάρκας αὐτῆς φάγονται, καὶ αὐτὴν κατακαύσουσιν πυρί·* 17 *ὁ γὰρ θεὸς ἔδωκεν εἰς τὰς καρδίας αὐτῶν ποιῆσαι τὴν γνώμην αὐτοῦ καὶ ποιῆσαι μίαν γνώμην καὶ δοῦναι τὴν βασιλείαν αὐτῶν τῷ θηρίῳ, ἄχρι τελεσθήσονται οἱ λόγοι τοῦ θεοῦ.* 18 *καὶ ἡ γυνὴ ἣν εἶδες ἔστιν ἡ πόλις ἡ μεγάλη ἡ ἔχουσα βασιλείαν ἐπὶ τῶν βασιλέων τῆς γῆς.*
1 *Μετὰ ταῦτα εἶδον ἄλλον ἄγγελον καταβαίνοντα ἐκ τοῦ οὐρανοῦ, ἔχοντα ἐξουσίαν μεγάλην, καὶ ἡ γῆ ἐφωτίσθη ἐκ τῆς δόξης αὐτοῦ.* 2 *καὶ ἔκραξεν ἐν ἰσχυρᾷ φωνῇ λέγων·* ἔπεσεν ἔπεσεν Βαβυλὼν ἡ μεγάλη, *καὶ ἐγένετο κατοικητήριον δαιμονίων καὶ φυλακὴ παντὸς πνεύματος ἀκαθάρτου καὶ φυλακὴ παντὸς ὀρνέου ἀκαθάρτου καὶ μεμισημένου,* 3 *ὅτι ἐκ τοῦ οἴνου τοῦ θυμοῦ τῆς πορνείας αὐτῆς πέπωκαν πάντα τὰ ἔθνη, καὶ οἱ βασιλεῖς τῆς γῆς μετ᾽ αὐτῆς ἐπόρνευσαν, καὶ οἱ ἔμποροι τῆς γῆς ἐκ τῆς δυνάμεως τοῦ στρήνους αὐτῆς ἐπλούτησαν.* 4 *καὶ ἤκουσα ἄλλην φωνὴν ἐκ τοῦ οὐρανοῦ λέγουσαν· ἐξέλθατε ὁ λαός μου ἐξ αὐτῆς, ἵνα μὴ συνκοινωνήσητε ταῖς ἁμαρτίαις αὐτῆς, καὶ ἐκ τῶν πληγῶν αὐτῆς ἵνα μὴ λάβητε,* 5 *ὅτι ἐκολλήθησαν αὐτῆς αἱ ἁμαρτίαι ἄχρι τοῦ οὐρανοῦ καὶ ἐμνημόνευσεν ὁ θεὸς τὰ ἀδικήματα αὐτῆς.* 6 *ἀπόδοτε αὐτῇ ὡς*

§ XIV

Disruption and Anarchy

xvii. 9 The seven heads are seven waters upon which the woman is seated. 10 And they are seven monarchies. The five have fallen, the one still is, the other has not yet come; and, when it is come, it is to endure a short time. 11 The beast which was and is not is also the eighth. It is from the seven[1]. 12 The ten horns which thou hast seen are ten kings who have not yet received dominion, but they shall receive as kings authority with the beast for one hour[2]. 13 These have one mind, which is to give their power and authority to the beast. 14 These shall fight with the Lamb, and the Lamb shall vanquish them because He is Lord of lords and King of kings, and those with Him are the elect, chosen and faithful[3]. 15 Then he says to me: The waters which thou hast seen, where the harlot is seated, are peoples and multitudes and nations and languages. 16 The ten horns which thou hast seen and the beast, these will hate the harlot and will make her waste and naked, and eat her flesh and burn her with fire[2]. 17 For God has put it into their hearts to work His purpose, to give with one mind their rule to the beast, till God's words shall be fulfilled. 18 And the woman whom thou hast seen is the Great City which has dominion over the kings of the earth. xviii. 1 Thereafter I saw another angel coming down from heaven, having great authority, and the earth was lighted up by his glory. 2 And he cried with a strong voice saying: Fallen, fallen is Babylon the Great! and is become a habitation of demons, a post of every unclean spirit and a post of every unclean and hateful bird[4]; 3 for from the wine of the anger of her fornication all the nations have drunk, and the kings of the earth have committed fornication with her, and the merchants of the earth been enriched from the wealth of her wantoning. 4 Then I heard another voice from heaven saying: Come out of her, my people, that ye do not participate in her sins and receive of her plagues, 5 for her sins have been piled up to heaven, and God has called to remembrance her iniquities. 6 Render

[1] Dan. vii. 23. The fourth beast shall be a fourth kingdom upon earth, which shall be diverse from all the kingdoms, and shall devour the whole earth and tread it down and break it in pieces. [2] vii. 24. And as for the ten horns, out of this kingdom shall ten kings arise. [3] vii. 21. The same horn made war with the saints, and prevailed against them until the ancient of days came. [4] Is. xxxiv. 8–15.

§ XV

Ch. xviii. 6–19

καὶ αὐτὴ ἀπέδωκεν, καὶ διπλώσατε τὰ διπλᾶ κατὰ τὰ ἔργα αὐτῆς· ἐν τῷ ποτηρίῳ ᾧ ἐκέρασεν κεράσατε αὐτῇ διπλοῦν· 7 ὅσα ἐδόξασεν αὐτὴν καὶ ἐστρηνίασεν, τοσοῦτον δότε αὐτῇ βασανισμὸν καὶ πένθος. ὅτι ἐν τῇ καρδίᾳ αὐτῆς λέγει ὅτι κάθημαι βασίλισσα καὶ χήρα οὐκ εἰμὶ καὶ πένθος οὐ μὴ ἴδω, 8 διὰ τοῦτο ἐν μιᾷ ἡμέρᾳ ἥξουσιν αἱ πληγαὶ αὐτῆς, θάνατος καὶ πένθος καὶ λιμός, καὶ ἐν πυρὶ κατακαυθήσεται· ὅτι ἰσχυρὸς κύριος ὁ θεὸς ὁ κρίνας αὐτήν. 9 καὶ κλαύσονται καὶ κόψονται ἐπ' αὐτὴν οἱ βασιλεῖς τῆς γῆς οἱ μετ' αὐτῆς πορνεύσαντες καὶ στρηνιάσαντες, ὅταν βλέπωσιν τὸν καπνὸν τῆς πυρώσεως αὐτῆς, 10 ἀπὸ μακρόθεν ἑστηκότες διὰ τὸν φόβον τοῦ βασανισμοῦ αὐτῆς, λέγοντες· οὐαὶ οὐαί, * Βαβυλὼν ἡ πόλις ἡ ἰσχυρά, ὅτι μιᾷ ὥρᾳ ἦλθεν ἡ κρίσις σου. 11 καὶ οἱ ἔμποροι τῆς γῆς κλαίουσιν καὶ πενθοῦσιν ἐπ' αὐτήν, ὅτι τὸν γόμον αὐτῶν οὐδεὶς ἀγοράζει οὐκέτι, 12 γόμον χρυσοῦ καὶ ἀργύρου καὶ λίθου τιμίου καὶ μαργαριτῶν καὶ βυσσίνου καὶ πορφύρας καὶ σιρικοῦ καὶ κοκκίνου, καὶ πᾶν ξύλον θύϊνον καὶ πᾶν σκεῦος ἐλεφάντινον καὶ πᾶν σκεῦος ἐκ ξύλου τιμιωτάτου καὶ χαλκοῦ καὶ σιδήρου καὶ μαρμάρου, 13 καὶ κιννάμωμον καὶ ἄμωμον καὶ θυμιάματα καὶ μύρον καὶ λίβανον καὶ οἶνον καὶ ἔλαιον καὶ σεμίδαλιν καὶ σῖτον καὶ κτήνη καὶ πρόβατα, καὶ ἵππων καὶ ῥεδῶν καὶ σωμάτων, καὶ ψυχὰς ἀνθρώπων, 14 καὶ ἡ ὀπώρα σου τῆς ἐπιθυμίας τῆς ψυχῆς ἀπῆλθεν ἀπὸ σοῦ, καὶ πάντα τὰ λιπαρὰ καὶ τὰ λαμπρὰ ἀπώλοντο ἀπὸ σοῦ, καὶ οὐκέτι οὐ μὴ αὐτὰ εὑρήσουσιν. 15 οἱ ἔμποροι τούτων, οἱ πλουτήσαντες ἀπ' αὐτῆς, * στήσονται κλαίοντες καὶ πενθοῦντες, 16 λέγοντες· οὐαὶ οὐαί, ἡ πόλις ἡ μεγάλη, ἡ περιβεβλημένη βύσσινον καὶ πορφυροῦν καὶ κόκκινον, καὶ κεχρυσωμένη ἐν χρυσῷ καὶ λίθῳ τιμίῳ καὶ μαργαρίτῃ, ὅτι μιᾷ ὥρᾳ ἠρημώθη ὁ τοσοῦτος πλοῦτος. 17 καὶ πᾶς κυβερνήτης καὶ πᾶς ὁ ἐπὶ τόπον πλέων καὶ ναῦται καὶ ὅσοι τὴν θάλασσαν ἐργάζονται, * 18 καὶ ἔκραζον * λέγοντες· τίς ὁμοία τῇ πόλει τῇ μεγάλῃ; 19 καὶ ἔβαλον χοῦν ἐπὶ τὰς κεφαλὰς αὐτῶν καὶ ἔκραζον κλαίοντες καὶ πενθοῦντες, λέγοντες· οὐαὶ οὐαί, ἡ πόλις ἡ μεγάλη, ἐν ᾗ ἐπλούτησαν

§ XV

Desolation and Mourning

xviii. 6 to her as she rendered, yea doubling twofold according to her works. In the cup which she mingled mix for her double[1]. 7 According as she glorified herself and wantoned give to her trial and grief, for in her heart she says: I am seated as a queen, I am no widow and grief shall I never see. 8 For this shall her plagues come in one day—pestilence and grief and famine—and with fire shall she be burned: because strong is the Lord God who has judged her. 9 Then shall the kings of the earth, who have committed fornication and wantoned with her, weep and wail over her, when they see the smoke of her burning. 10 Having taken their stand afar off for fear of her torment, they shall say: Woe, woe, Babylon the strong city! for in one hour thy judgment has come. 11 Over her the merchants of the earth weep and grieve, because no one any more buys their lading—12 lading of gold and silver and precious stone and pearls and fine linen and purple and silk and scarlet, and every kind of thyine wood, or of ivory vessel, or of vessel of precious wood or brass or iron or marble, 13 or cinnamon or spice or incense or perfume, or frankincense or wine or oil, or fine flour or wheat, or cattle or sheep, or of horses or chariots or slaves, yea lives of men. 14 The fruit of thy soul's desire has gone from thee. All that is soft and all that is bright are lost utterly from thee, never any more shall they be found. 15 The merchants of these things, they who became rich by her shall stand, weeping and grieving, 16 saying: Woe, woe, the Great City, once arrayed in fine linen and purple and scarlet, decked in gold and precious stone and pearl. For in one hour wealth so great has been reft away. 17 Every steersman and every one sailing towards a place, and sailors, yea whosoever live by the sea, 18 cried out saying: What *city* is like the Great City! 19 And they cast dust on their heads and cried out, weeping and grieving, saying: Woe, woe the city, the Great City whereby were enriched

[1] Jer. xvi. 18. I will recompense their iniquity and their sin double. xvii. 18. And destroy them with double destruction.

§ XVI

Ch. xviii. 19—xix. 9

πάντες οἱ ἔχοντες τὰ πλοῖα ἐν τῇ θαλάσσῃ ἐκ τῆς τιμιότητος αὐτῆς, ὅτι μιᾷ ὥρᾳ ἠρημώθη. 20 εὐφραίνου ἐπ' αὐτῇ, οὐρανὲ καὶ οἱ ἅγιοι καὶ οἱ ἀπόστολοι καὶ οἱ προφῆται, ὅτι ἔκρινεν ὁ θεὸς τὸ κρίμα ὑμῶν ἐξ αὐτῆς. 21 καὶ ἦρεν εἷς ἄγγελος ἰσχυρὸς λίθον ὡς μῦλον μέγαν, καὶ ἔβαλεν εἰς τὴν θάλασσαν λέγων· οὕτως ὁρμήματι βληθήσεται Βαβυλὼν ἡ μεγάλη πόλις, καὶ οὐ μὴ εὑρεθῇ ἔτι. 22 καὶ φωνὴ κιθαρῳδῶν καὶ μουσικῶν καὶ αὐλητῶν καὶ σαλπιστῶν οὐ μὴ ἀκουσθῇ ἐν σοὶ ἔτι, καὶ πᾶς τεχνίτης πάσης τέχνης οὐ μὴ εὑρεθῇ ἐν σοὶ ἔτι, καὶ φωνὴ μύλου οὐ μὴ ἀκουσθῇ ἐν σοὶ ἔτι, 23 καὶ φῶς λύχνου οὐ μὴ φανῇ ἐν σοὶ ἔτι, καὶ φωνὴ νυμφίου καὶ νύμφης οὐ μὴ ἀκουσθῇ ἐν σοὶ ἔτι, ὅτι οἱ ἔμποροί σου ἦσαν οἱ μεγιστᾶνες τῆς γῆς, ὅτι ἐν τῇ φαρμακίᾳ σοῦ ἐπλανήθησαν πάντα τὰ ἔθνη, 24 καὶ ἐν αὐτῇ αἵματα προφητῶν καὶ ἁγίων εὑρέθη καὶ πάντων τῶν ἐσφαγμένων ἐπὶ τῆς γῆς. 1 Μετὰ ταῦτα ἤκουσα ὡς φωνὴν μεγάλην ὄχλου πολλοῦ ἐν τῷ οὐρανῷ λεγόντων· ἀλληλούϊα, ἡ σωτηρία καὶ ἡ δόξα καὶ ἡ δύναμις τοῦ θεοῦ ἡμῶν, 2 ὅτι ἀληθιναὶ καὶ δίκαιαι αἱ κρίσεις αὐτοῦ, ὅτι ἔκρινεν τὴν πόρνην τὴν μεγάλην ἥτις ἔφθειρεν τὴν γῆν ἐν τῇ πορνείᾳ αὐτῆς, καὶ ἐξεδίκησεν τὸ αἷμα τῶν δούλων αὐτοῦ ἐκ χειρὸς αὐτῆς. 3 καὶ δεύτερον εἴρηκαν· ἀλληλούϊα, καὶ ὁ καπνὸς αὐτῆς ἀναβαίνει εἰς τοὺς αἰῶνας τῶν αἰώνων. 4 καὶ ἔπεσαν οἱ πρεσβύτεροι οἱ εἴκοσι τέσσαρες καὶ τὰ τέσσερα ζῷα, καὶ προσεκύνησαν τῷ θεῷ τῷ καθημένῳ ἐπὶ τῷ θρόνῳ λέγοντες· ἀμὴν ἀλληλούϊα. 5 καὶ φωνὴ ἐκ τοῦ θρόνου ἐξῆλθεν λέγουσα· αἰνεῖτε τῷ θεῷ ἡμῶν, πάντες οἱ δοῦλοι αὐτοῦ, οἱ φοβούμενοι αὐτόν. * 6 καὶ ἤκουσα ὡς φωνὴν ὄχλου πολλοῦ καὶ ὡς φωνὴν ὑδάτων πολλῶν καὶ ὡς φωνὴν βροντῶν ἰσχυρῶν, λεγόντων· ἀλληλούϊα, ὅτι ἐβασίλευσεν κύριος ὁ θεὸς ἡμῶν ὁ παντοκράτωρ. 7 χαίρωμεν καὶ ἀγαλλιῶμεν, καὶ δῶμεν τὴν δόξαν αὐτῷ, ὅτι ἦλθεν ὁ γάμος τοῦ ἀρνίου καὶ ἡ γυνὴ αὐτοῦ ἡτοίμασεν ἑαυτήν, 8 καὶ ἐδόθη αὐτῇ ἵνα περιβάληται βύσσινον λαμπρὸν καθαρόν. τὸ γὰρ βύσσινον τὰ δικαιώματα τῶν ἁγίων ἐστίν. 9 καὶ λέγει μοι· γράψον· μακάριοι οἱ εἰς τὸ δεῖπνον τοῦ γάμου τοῦ ἀρνίου κεκλημένοι.

§ XVI

THE OLD ORDER AND THE NEW

xviii. 19 all having ships on the sea, even from her costliness! For in one hour she has been laid waste. 20 Rejoice over her, O heaven and ye saints and apostles and prophets, because God has judged your judgment on her. 21 Then a strong angel raised a stone like a great mill-stone and cast it into the sea, saying: Thus, with an impulsion shall Babylon the Great City be hurled down, and be found no more. 22 Note of harpers shall never more be heard in thee, nor of minstrels or flute-players or trumpeters, nor in thee ever more be found any craftsman of any trade. Never in thee again shall sound of mill-stone be heard, 23 nor light of lamp ever shine, nor voice of bridegroom or bride ever again be heard[1]. For thy merchants were the magnates of the earth, and by thy enchantment all nations were deceived. 24 In her the blood of prophets and saints was found, yea of all slain upon the earth. xix. 1 Thereafter I heard as it were a great voice of a vast multitude in heaven saying: Hallelujah, the salvation and the glory and the power of our God! 2 for true and righteous are His judgments. For He has judged the great harlot who has destroyed the earth with her fornication, and exacted at her hand justice for the blood of His servants. 3 And once again they said: Hallelujah. Her smoke goes up for ages of ages[2]. 4 Then the twenty-four elders and the four living creatures fell down and worshipped the God who sits on the throne, saying: Amen, Hallelujah. 5 Then a voice came forth from the throne, saying: Praise our God, all His servants, those who fear Him. 6 Then, like the sound of a vast multitude, like the sound of many waters, like the sound of heavy thunders, I heard them saying: Hallelujah! for the All-sovereign Lord our God now reigns. 7 Let us rejoice and exult and give Him the glory, because the marriage of the Lamb has come, and His wife has made herself ready, 8 and it has been granted her that she be clothed in fine linen, bright and pure, the linen being the righteous doings of the saints[3]. 9 And he says to me, write: Blessed are those who are called to the marriage-supper of the Lamb[4].

[1] Jer. xxv. 10. Moreover I will take from them the voice of mirth, etc. [2] Is. xxxiv. 10. It shall not be quenched night nor day; the smoke thereof shall go up for ever: from generation to generation it shall lie waste. [3] Is. lii. 1. Awake, awake, put on thy strength, O Zion: put on thy beautiful garments, O Jerusalem, the holy city; for henceforth there shall no more come into thee the uncircumcised and the unclean. lx. i. Arise, shine; for thy light has come, and the glory of the Lord is risen upon thee. [4] Lk. xiv. 15. Blessed is he that shall eat bread in the kingdom of God...a certain man made a great supper, and he bade many. Mt. xxii. 2. The kingdom of heaven is likened unto a certain king, who made a marriage feast for his son.

§ XVII

Ch. i. 7, iv. i—v. 2

7 Ἰδού, *ἔρχεται μετὰ τῶν νεφελῶν, καὶ ὄψεται αὐτὸν πᾶς ὀφθαλμὸς καὶ οἵτινες αὐτὸν ἐξεκέντησαν, καὶ κόψονται ἐπ' αὐτὸν πᾶσαι αἱ φυλαὶ τῆς γῆς*. 1 μετὰ ταῦτα ἴδον καὶ ἰδοὺ θύρα ἠνεῳγμένη ἐν τῷ οὐρανῷ, καὶ ἡ φωνὴ ἡ πρώτη ἣν ἤκουσα ὡς σάλπιγγος λαλούσης μετ' ἐμοῦ, λέγων· ἀνάβα ὧδε, καὶ δείξω σοι ἃ δεῖ γενέσθαι μετὰ ταῦτα. 2 εὐθέως ἐγενόμην ἐν πνεύματι· καὶ ἰδοὺ θρόνος ἔκειτο ἐν τῷ οὐρανῷ, καὶ ἐπὶ τὸν θρόνον καθήμενος, 3 καὶ ὁ καθήμενος ὅμοιος ὁράσει λίθῳ ἰάσπιδι καὶ σαρδίῳ, καὶ ἶρις κυκλόθεν τοῦ θρόνου ὅμοιος ὁράσει σμαραγδίνῳ. 4 καὶ κυκλόθεν τοῦ θρόνου θρόνους εἴκοσι τέσσαρας, καὶ ἐπὶ τοὺς θρόνους εἴκοσι τέσσαρας πρεσβυτέρους καθημένους περιβεβλημένους ἐν ἱματίοις λευκοῖς, καὶ ἐπὶ τὰς κεφαλὰς αὐτῶν στεφάνους χρυσοῦς. 5 καὶ ἐκ τοῦ θρόνου ἐκπορεύονται ἀστραπαί· * καὶ ἑπτὰ λαμπάδες πυρὸς καιόμεναι ἐνώπιον τοῦ θρόνου, ἅ εἰσιν τὰ ἑπτὰ πνεύματα τοῦ θεοῦ· 6 καὶ ἐνώπιον τοῦ θρόνου ὡς θάλασσα ὑαλίνη ὁμοία κρυστάλλῳ· καὶ ἐν μέσῳ τοῦ θρόνου καὶ κύκλῳ τοῦ θρόνου τέσσερα ζῷα γέμοντα ὀφθαλμῶν ἔμπροσθεν καὶ ὄπισθεν. 7 καὶ τὸ ζῷον τὸ πρῶτον ὅμοιον λέοντι, καὶ τὸ δεύτερον ζῷον ὅμοιον μόσχῳ, καὶ τὸ τρίτον ζῷον ἔχων τὸ πρόσωπον ὡς ἀνθρώπου, καὶ τὸ τέταρτον ζῷον ὅμοιον ἀετῷ πετομένῳ. 8 καὶ τὰ τέσσερα ζῷα, ἓν καθ' ἓν αὐτῶν ἔχων ἀνὰ πτέρυγας ἕξ, κυκλόθεν καὶ ἔσωθεν γέμουσιν ὀφθαλμῶν, καὶ ἀνάπαυσιν οὐκ ἔχουσιν ἡμέρας καὶ νυκτὸς λέγοντες· *ἅγιος ἅγιος ἅγιος κύριος ὁ θεὸς ὁ παντοκράτωρ* ὁ ἦν καὶ ὁ ὢν καὶ ὁ ἐρχόμενος. 9 καὶ ὅταν δώσουσιν τὰ ζῷα δόξαν καὶ τιμὴν καὶ εὐχαριστίαν, * 10 πεσοῦνται οἱ εἴκοσι τέσσαρες πρεσβύτεροι ἐνώπιον τοῦ καθημένου ἐπὶ τοῦ θρόνου, καὶ προσκυνήσουσιν τῷ ζῶντι εἰς τοὺς αἰῶνας τῶν αἰώνων, καὶ βαλοῦσιν τοὺς στεφάνους αὐτῶν ἐνώπιον τοῦ θρόνου, λέγοντες· 11 ἄξιος εἶ, ὁ κύριος καὶ ὁ θεὸς ἡμῶν, λαβεῖν τὴν δόξαν καὶ τὴν τιμὴν καὶ τὴν δύναμιν, ὅτι σὺ ἔκτισας τὰ πάντα, καὶ διὰ τὸ θέλημά σου ἦσαν καὶ ἐκτίσθησαν. 1 καὶ εἶδον ἐπὶ τὴν δεξιὰν τοῦ καθημένου ἐπὶ τοῦ θρόνου βιβλίον γεγραμμένον ἔσωθεν καὶ ὄπισθεν, κατεσφραγισμένον σφραγῖσιν ἑπτά. 2 καὶ εἶδον

§ XVII

The New Prophetic Source

i. 7 Lo He comes with the clouds, and every eye shall see Him, and those who pierced Him, and all the tribes of the earth shall wail because of Him. iv. 1 After these things I saw, and lo a door opened in heaven, and the first voice which I heard as of a trumpet speaking with me saying: Come up hither, and I will show thee what must come to pass after these things. 2 Straightway I was in the spirit, and lo a throne was set in heaven; and sitting on the throne 3 was one like in appearance to a jasper stone and a sardius, and the rainbow round about the throne was like in appearance to an emerald[1]. 4 Around the throne were twenty-four thrones, and on the thrones twenty-four elders sitting clothed in white garments, and on their heads golden crowns. 5 From the throne go forth lightnings, and before the throne are burning seven torches of fire, which are the seven spirits of God[2]. 6 Also before the throne as it were a glassy sea like crystal[3]. In the midst of the throne and round about the throne four living creatures, full of eyes before and behind—7 the first living creature being like a lion, the second like a young bull, the third having its face like a man's, and the fourth being like a flying eagle. 8 Each of the four living creatures had six wings, outside and inside full of eyes[4]. Without ceasing day and night they say: Holy, holy, holy Lord, the All-sovereign God, who was, who is, and is to be[5]. 9 And whensoever the living creatures give glory and honour and thanks, 10 the twenty-four elders will fall down before Him who sits on the throne and worship Him who is the living one to ages of ages and cast their crowns before the throne saying: 11 Worthy art Thou, Lord and our God, to receive the glory and the honour and the power, because Thou hast created all things, and by Thy will they were, and were created. v. 1 Then I saw on the right hand of Him who was sitting on the throne, a roll written within and without, sealed with seven seals. 2 And I saw

[1] Ez. i. 26 ff. And above the firmament that was over their heads, was the likeness of a throne as the appearance of a sapphire stone...a likeness as the appearance of a man upon it above. And I saw as the colour of amber as the appearance of fire...and there was brightness round about him. As the appearance of the bow that is in the cloud....This was the appearance of the likeness of the glory of the Lord. [2] Dan. x. 6. His eyes as lamps of fire. Is. iii. 8. The eyes of his glory. [3] 1 K. vii. 23. He made a molten sea. Ez. i. 22. A firmament like the colour of the terrible crystal. [4] Ez. i. 10. They had the face of a man; and the four had the face of a lion on the right side; and the four had the face of an ox on the left side; the four had also the face of an eagle. *v.* 18. And they four had their rings full of eyes round about. [5] Is. vi. 1. The Lord sitting upon a throne high and lifted up...seraphim: each one had six wings and said Holy, holy, holy is the Lord of hosts: the whole earth is full of his glory.

§ XVIII

Ch. v. 2—vi. 1.

ἄγγελον ἰσχυρὸν κηρύσσοντα ἐν φωνῇ μεγάλῃ· τίς ἄξιος ἀνοῖξαι τὸ βιβλίον καὶ λῦσαι τὰς σφραγῖδας αὐτοῦ; 3 καὶ οὐδεὶς ἐδύνατο ἐν τῷ οὐρανῷ οὔτε ἐπὶ τῆς γῆς οὔτε ὑποκάτω τῆς γῆς ἀνοῖξαι τὸ βιβλίον οὔτε βλέπειν αὐτό. 4 καὶ ἔκλαιον πολύ, ὅτι οὐδεὶς ἄξιος εὑρέθη ἀνοῖξαι τὸ βιβλίον οὔτε βλέπειν αὐτό. 5 καὶ εἷς ἐκ τῶν πρεσβυτέρων λέγει μοι· μὴ κλαῖε· ἰδοὺ ἐνίκησεν ὁ λέων ὁ ἐκ τῆς φυλῆς Ἰούδα, ἡ ῥίζα Δαυείδ, ἀνοῖξαι τὸ βιβλίον καὶ τὰς ἑπτὰ σφραγῖδας αὐτοῦ. 6 Καὶ εἶδον ἐν μέσῳ τοῦ θρόνου καὶ τῶν τεσσάρων ζώων καὶ ἐν μέσῳ τῶν πρεσβυτέρων ἀρνίον ἑστηκὼς ὡς ἐσφαγμένον, ἔχων κέρατα ἑπτὰ καὶ ὀφθαλμοὺς ἑπτά, οἵ εἰσιν τὰ ἑπτὰ πνεύματα τοῦ θεοῦ ἀπεσταλμένα εἰς πᾶσαν τὴν γῆν. 7 καὶ ἦλθεν καὶ εἴληφεν ἐκ τῆς δεξιᾶς τοῦ καθημένου ἐπὶ τοῦ θρόνου. 8 καὶ ὅτε ἔλαβεν τὸ βιβλίον, τὰ τέσσερα ζῶα καὶ οἱ εἴκοσι τέσσαρες πρεσβύτεροι ἔπεσαν ἐνώπιον τοῦ ἀρνίου, ἔχοντες ἕκαστος κιθάραν καὶ φιάλας χρυσᾶς γεμούσας θυμιαμάτων, ἅ εἰσιν αἱ προσευχαὶ τῶν ἁγίων. 9 καὶ ᾄδουσιν ᾠδὴν καινὴν λέγοντες· ἄξιος εἶ λαβεῖν τὸ βιβλίον καὶ ἀνοῖξαι τὰς σφραγῖδας αὐτοῦ, ὅτι ἐσφάγης καὶ ἠγόρασας τῷ θεῷ ἐν τῷ αἵματί σου ἐκ πάσης φυλῆς καὶ γλώσσης καὶ λαοῦ καὶ ἔθνους, 10 καὶ ἐποίησας αὐτοὺς τῷ θεῷ ἡμῶν βασιλείαν καὶ ἱερεῖς, καὶ βασιλεύσουσιν ἐπὶ τῆς γῆς. 11 καὶ εἶδον, καὶ ἤκουσα ὡς φωνὴν ἀγγέλων πολλῶν κύκλῳ τοῦ θρόνου καὶ τῶν ζώων καὶ τῶν πρεσβυτέρων, καὶ ἦν ὁ ἀριθμὸς αὐτῶν μυριάδες μυριάδων καὶ χιλιάδες χιλιάδων, 12 λέγοντες φωνῇ μεγάλῃ· ἄξιός ἐστιν τὸ ἀρνίον τὸ ἐσφαγμένον λαβεῖν τὴν δύναμιν καὶ πλοῦτον καὶ σοφίαν καὶ ἰσχὺν καὶ τιμὴν καὶ δόξαν καὶ εὐλογίαν. 13 καὶ πᾶν κτίσμα ὃ ἐν τῷ οὐρανῷ καὶ ἐπὶ τῆς γῆς καὶ ὑποκάτω τῆς γῆς καὶ ἐπὶ τῆς θαλάσσης καὶ τὰ ἐν αὐτοῖς πάντα καὶ ἤκουσα λέγοντας· τῷ καθημένῳ ἐπὶ τῷ θρόνῳ καὶ τῷ ἀρνίῳ ἡ εὐλογία καὶ ἡ τιμὴ καὶ ἡ δόξα καὶ τὸ κράτος εἰς τοὺς αἰῶνας τῶν αἰώνων. 14 καὶ τὰ τέσσερα ζῶα ἔλεγον· ἀμήν, καὶ οἱ πρεσβύτεροι ἔπεσαν καὶ προσεκύνησαν. 1 Καὶ ἴδον ὅτε ἤνοιξεν τὸ ἀρνίον μίαν ἐκ τῶν ἑπτὰ σφραγίδων, καὶ ἤκουσα ἑνὸς ἐκ τῶν τεσσάρων ζώων λέγοντος ὡς φωνὴ βροντῆς· ἔρχου καὶ βλέπε[1].

[1] Omitted in Geb.

§ XVIII

THE ROLL AND THE LAMB

v. 2 a strong angel proclaiming with a great voice: Who is worthy to open the roll and undo the seals of it? 3 But no one in heaven or on earth or under the earth was able to open the book or see into it. 4 Then I wept sore that no one was found worthy to open the roll or see into it[1]. 5 But one of the elders says to me: Do not weep. Lo the lion who is of the tribe of Judah[2], *He who is* the root of David[3], has prevailed to open the roll, even its seven seals. 6 Then I saw in the midst of the throne and of the four living creatures, and in the midst of the elders, a Lamb standing. It was as though He had been slain[4]; and He had seven horns and seven eyes which are the seven spirits of God sent forth unto all the earth[5]. 7 He came and took from the right hand of Him who was sitting on the throne. 8 And when He had taken the roll, the four living creatures and the twenty-four elders fell before the Lamb, each having a harp and golden vials full of incense, which is the prayers of the saints[6]. 9 And they sing a new song saying: Worthy art Thou to receive the roll and to open its seals, because Thou wast slain and hast purchased to God with Thy blood some from every tribe, language, people and nation, 10 and made them to our God a kingdom and priests, and they shall reign on the earth[7]. 11 Then I saw, and heard as it were a voice of many angels round about the throne and the living creatures and the elders, and their number was myriads of myriads and thousands of thousands, 12 saying with a great voice: Worthy is the Lamb, he who was slain, to receive the might and riches and wisdom and strength and honour and glory and praise. 13 And every creature that is in heaven and on the earth and under the earth and on the sea, and all that in them is I heard saying: To Him that sitteth on the throne and to the Lamb be the praise and the honour and the glory and the power to ages of ages. 14 And the four living creatures said: Amen, and the elders fell down and worshipped. vi. 1 And I saw, when the Lamb had opened one of the seven seals, and I heard one of the living creatures saying like a sound of thunder: Come and see[8].

[1] Dan. xii. 1. At that time thy people shall be delivered, every one that shall be found written in the book. [2] Gen. xlix. 9, 10. Judah is a lion's whelp...until Shiloh come; and unto him shall the obedience of the people be. [3] Is. xi. 10. The root of Jesse, which standeth for an ensign of the peoples. [4] Is. liii. 7. As a lamb that is led to the slaughter. [5] Dan. x. 6. His eyes like lamps of fire. Cf. Rev. iv. 5 (§ XVII) and 2 Chron. xvi. 9. For the eyes of the Lord run to and fro throughout the whole earth. [6] Ps. cxli. 2. Let my prayer be set forth as incense before thee. [7] Dan. vii. 10. Thousand thousands ministered unto him and ten thousand times ten thousand stood before him. *v.* 14. There was given him dominion and glory and a kingdom. 1 Pet. ii. 9. A royal priesthood. [8] Rom. viii. 19. For the earnest expectation of the creation waiteth for the revealing of the sons of God.

§ XIX

Ch. vi. 2–17

2 καὶ ἴδον, καὶ ἰδοὺ ἵππος λευκός, καὶ ὁ καθήμενος ἐπ᾽ αὐτὸν ἔχων τόξον, καὶ ἐδόθη αὐτῷ στέφανος, καὶ ἐξῆλθεν νικῶν καὶ ἵνα νικήσῃ. * 4 καὶ ἐξῆλθεν ἄλλος ἵππος πυρρός, καὶ τῷ καθημένῳ ἐπ᾽ αὐτὸν ἐδόθη αὐτῷ λαβεῖν τὴν εἰρήνην ἐκ τῆς γῆς καὶ ἵνα ἀλλήλους σφάξουσιν, καὶ ἐδόθη αὐτῷ μάχαιρα μεγάλη. 5 * καὶ ἴδον, καὶ ἰδοὺ ἵππος μέλας, καὶ ὁ καθήμενος ἐπ᾽ αὐτὸν ἔχων ζυγὸν ἐν τῇ χειρὶ αὐτοῦ. 6 καὶ ἤκουσα ὡς φωνὴν ἐν μέσῳ τῶν τεσσάρων ζώων λέγουσαν· χοῖνιξ σίτου δηναρίου, καὶ τρεῖς χοίνικες κριθῶν δηναρίου· καὶ τὸ ἔλαιον καὶ τὸν οἶνον μὴ ἀδικήσῃς. * 8 καὶ ἴδον, καὶ ἰδοὺ ἵππος χλωρός, καὶ ὁ καθήμενος ἐπάνω αὐτοῦ, ὄνομα αὐτῷ θάνατος, καὶ ὁ ᾅδης ἠκολούθει μετ᾽ αὐτοῦ, καὶ ἐδόθη αὐτοῖς ἐξουσία ἐπὶ τὸ τέταρτον τῆς γῆς, ἀποκτεῖναι ἐν ῥομφαίᾳ καὶ ἐν λιμῷ καὶ ἐν θανάτῳ καὶ ὑπὸ τῶν θηρίων τῆς γῆς. 9 * καὶ ἴδον ὑποκάτω τοῦ θυσιαστηρίου τὰς ψυχὰς τῶν ἐσφαγμένων διὰ τὸν λόγον τοῦ θεοῦ καὶ διὰ τὴν μαρτυρίαν ἣν εἶχον. 10 καὶ ἔκραξαν φωνῇ μεγάλῃ λέγοντες· ἕως πότε, ὁ δεσπότης ὁ ἅγιος καὶ ἀληθινός, οὐ κρίνεις καὶ ἐκδικεῖς τὸ αἷμα ἡμῶν ἐκ τῶν κατοικούντων ἐπὶ τῆς γῆς; 11 καὶ ἐδόθη αὐτοῖς ἑκάστῳ στολὴ λευκή, καὶ ἐρρέθη αὐτοῖς ἵνα ἀναπαύσωνται ἔτι χρόνον μικρόν, ἕως πληρώσωσιν καὶ οἱ σύνδουλοι αὐτῶν καὶ οἱ ἀδελφοὶ αὐτῶν οἱ μέλλοντες ἀποκτέννεσθαι ὡς καὶ αὐτοί. 12 * καὶ ἴδον, καὶ σεισμὸς μέγας ἐγένετο, καὶ ὁ ἥλιος μέλας ἐγένετο ὡς σάκκος τρίχινος, καὶ ἡ σελήνη ὅλη ἐγένετο ὡς αἷμα, 13 καὶ οἱ ἀστέρες τοῦ οὐρανοῦ ἔπεσαν εἰς τὴν γῆν, ὡς συκῆ βάλλουσα τοὺς ὀλύνθους αὐτῆς ὑπὸ ἀνέμου μεγάλου σειομένη, 14 καὶ ὁ οὐρανὸς ἀπεχωρίσθη ὡς βιβλίον ἑλισσόμενον, καὶ πᾶν ὄρος καὶ νῆσος ἐκ τῶν τόπων αὐτῶν ἐκινήθησαν. 15 καὶ οἱ βασιλεῖς τῆς γῆς καὶ οἱ μεγιστᾶνες καὶ οἱ χιλίαρχοι καὶ οἱ πλούσιοι καὶ οἱ ἰσχυροὶ καὶ πᾶς δοῦλος καὶ ἐλεύθερος ἔκρυψαν ἑαυτοὺς εἰς τὰ σπήλαια καὶ εἰς τὰς πέτρας τῶν ὀρέων, 16 καὶ λέγουσιν τοῖς ὄρεσιν καὶ ταῖς πέτραις· πέσετε ἐφ᾽ ἡμᾶς καὶ κρύψατε ἡμᾶς ἀπὸ προσώπου τοῦ καθημένου ἐπὶ τῷ θρόνῳ καὶ ἀπὸ τῆς ὀργῆς τοῦ αὐτοῦ[1]. 17 ὅτι ἦλθεν ἡ ἡμέρα ἡ μεγάλη τῆς ὀργῆς αὐτῶν, καὶ τίς δύναται σταθῆναι;

[1] Geb. ἀρνίου.

§ XIX

Summary of the Woes

vi. 2 Then I saw, and lo a white horse and he who was sitting on him had a bow. And a crown was given him, and as a conqueror he went forth to conquer. 4 Then came forth another horse, a red one; and to the rider on him was it given to take peace from the earth, that men might slay each other. To him was given a great sword. 5 Then I saw, and lo a black horse, the rider on him having a balance in his hand. 6 And I heard a voice in the midst of the four living creatures saying: A quart of wheat for a day's wage and three quarts of barley for a day's wage. But injure not the olive and the vine. 8 Then I saw, and lo a pale horse, and his rider's name was Pestilence. And with him followed Hades. To these authority was given over a quarter of the earth to kill with sword, famine and pestilence, and by the wild beasts of the earth[1]. 9 Then I saw under the altar the souls of those slain on account of the word of God and for the witness which they held. 10 And they cried with a great voice saying: How long, O Sovereign, the holy and true, dost Thou not judge and take retribution for our blood from those who dwell on the earth? 11 Then to each of them a white robe was given, and it was told them that they must wait yet a little time until the number of their fellow servants and brethren, who are to be slain even as they, shall be full. 12 Then I saw, and there was a great earthquake and the sun became black as sackcloth of hair and the whole moon became as blood[2], 13 and the stars of the heavens fell to earth like a fig-tree shaken by a great wind casting its winter figs, 14 and the heavens were removed as a scroll being rolled up[3], and every mountain and island were removed from their places[4]. 15 The kings of the earth, and the magnates and the captains and the rich and the powerful, and slave and free-man alike, hid themselves in the caves and the rocks of the mountains[5]; 16 and they say to the mountains and to the rocks: Fall on us and hide us from the face of Him, who sits on the throne, and from the wrath of the Lamb, 17 because the great day of His wrath has come; and who is able to stand[6]?

[1] Zech. i. 8. A man riding on a red horse...and behind him there were horses, red, sorrel and white. [2] Joel ii. 30, 31. And I will show wonders in the heavens and the earth, blood and fire and pillars of smoke. The sun shall be turned into darkness and the moon into blood before the great and terrible day of the Lord come. [3] Is. xxxiv. 4. The heavens shall be rolled together as a scroll. [4] Is. xl. 4. Every mountain and hill shall be made low. [5] Is. ii. 9. And the mean man is bowed down and the great man is brought low. *v.* 19. And men shall go into the caves of the rocks and into the holes of the earth. [6] Lk. xxiii. 30. Then shall they begin to say to the mountains, fall on us, and to the hills, cover us.

§ XX

Ch. vii. 1–17

1 Καὶ μετὰ τοῦτο ἴδον τέσσαρας ἀγγέλους ἑστῶτας ἐπὶ τὰς τέσσαρας γωνίας τῆς γῆς, κρατοῦντας τοὺς τέσσαρας ἀνέμους τῆς γῆς, ἵνα μὴ πνέῃ ἄνεμος ἐπὶ τῆς γῆς μήτε ἐπὶ τῆς θαλάσσης μήτε ἐπὶ πᾶν δένδρον. 2 καὶ ἴδον ἄλλον ἄγγελον ἀναβαίνοντα ἀπὸ ἀνατολῆς ἡλίου, ἔχοντα σφραγῖδα θεοῦ ζῶντος, καὶ ἔκραξεν φωνῇ μεγάλῃ τοῖς τέσσαρσιν ἀγγέλοις,* 3 λέγων· μὴ ἀδικήσητε τὴν γῆν μήτε τὴν θάλασσαν μήτε τὰ δένδρα, ἄχρι σφραγίσωμεν τοὺς δούλους τοῦ θεοῦ ἡμῶν ἐπὶ τῶν μετώπων αὐτῶν. 4 καὶ ἤκουσα τὸν ἀριθμὸν τῶν ἐσφραγισμένων, ἑκατὸν τεσσεράκοντα τέσσαρες χιλιάδες ἐσφραγισμένοι ἐκ πάσης φυλῆς υἱῶν Ἰσραήλ.* 9 Μετὰ ταῦτα ἴδον, καὶ ἰδοὺ ὄχλος πολύς, ὃν ἀριθμῆσαι αὐτὸν οὐδεὶς ἐδύνατο, ἐκ παντὸς ἔθνους καὶ φυλῶν καὶ λαῶν καὶ γλωσσῶν, ἑστῶτες ἐνώπιον τοῦ θρόνου καὶ ἐνώπιον τοῦ ἀρνίου, περιβεβλημένους στολὰς λευκάς, καὶ φοίνικας ἐν ταῖς χερσὶν αὐτῶν· 10 καὶ κράζουσιν φωνῇ μεγάλῃ λέγοντες· ἡ σωτηρία τῷ θεῷ ἡμῶν τῷ καθημένῳ ἐπὶ τῷ θρόνῳ καὶ τῷ ἀρνίῳ. 11 καὶ πάντες οἱ ἄγγελοι εἱστήκεισαν κύκλῳ τοῦ θρόνου καὶ τῶν πρεσβυτέρων καὶ τῶν τεσσάρων ζώων, καὶ ἔπεσαν ἐνώπιον τοῦ θρόνου ἐπὶ τὰ πρόσωπα αὐτῶν καὶ προσεκύνησαν τῷ θεῷ, 12 λέγοντες· ἀμήν, ἡ εὐλογία καὶ ἡ δόξα καὶ ἡ σοφία καὶ ἡ εὐχαριστία καὶ ἡ τιμὴ καὶ ἡ δύναμις καὶ ἡ ἰσχὺς τῷ θεῷ ἡμῶν εἰς τοὺς αἰῶνας τῶν αἰώνων, ἀμήν. 13 καὶ ἀπεκρίθη εἷς ἐκ τῶν πρεσβυτέρων λέγων μοι· οὗτοι οἱ περιβεβλημένοι τὰς στολὰς τὰς λευκὰς τίνες εἰσὶν καὶ πόθεν ἦλθον; 14 καὶ εἴρηκα αὐτῷ· κύριέ μου, σὺ οἶδας. καὶ εἶπέν μοι· οὗτοί εἰσιν οἱ ἐρχόμενοι ἐκ τῆς θλίψεως τῆς μεγάλης, καὶ ἔπλυναν τὰς στολὰς αὐτῶν καὶ ἐλεύκαναν αὐτὰς ἐν τῷ αἵματι τοῦ ἀρνίου. 15 διὰ τοῦτό εἰσιν ἐνώπιον τοῦ θρόνου τοῦ θεοῦ, καὶ λατρεύουσιν αὐτῷ ἡμέρας καὶ νυκτὸς ἐν τῷ ναῷ αὐτοῦ, καὶ ὁ καθήμενος ἐπὶ τοῦ θρόνου σκηνώσει ἐπ' αὐτούς. 16 οὐ πεινάσουσιν ἔτι οὐδὲ διψήσουσιν ἔτι, οὐδὲ μὴ πέσῃ ἐπ' αὐτοὺς ὁ ἥλιος οὐδὲ πᾶν καῦμα, 17 ὅτι τὸ ἀρνίον τὸ ἀνὰ μέσον τοῦ θρόνου ποιμανεῖ αὐτοὺς καὶ ὁδηγήσει αὐτοὺς ἐπὶ ζωῆς πηγὰς ὑδάτων, καὶ ἐξαλείψει ὁ θεὸς πᾶν δάκρυον ἐκ τῶν ὀφθαλμῶν αὐτῶν.

§ XX

The Sealing of the Saints

vii. 1 Thereafter I saw four angels standing on the four corners of the earth[1], holding the four winds of the earth, that the wind may not blow on the earth or on the sea or on any tree[2]. 2 Then I saw another angel coming up from the east, having a seal of the living God, and he cried with a great voice to the four angels, 3 saying: Hurt not the earth, nor the sea, nor the trees, till we have sealed the servants of our God on their foreheads[3]. 4 And I heard the number of the sealed, a hundred and forty-four thousand, the sealed of every tribe of the sons of Israel. 9 Thereafter I saw, and lo a great multitude which no one could number, from every nation and tribe and people and language, standing before the throne and before the Lamb, clothed in white robes and palms in their hands. 10 And they shout with a great voice saying: The salvation is our God's, who sits on the throne, and the Lamb's! 11 And all the angels were standing round about the throne and the elders and the four living creatures, and they fell before the throne on their faces and worshipped God, 12 saying: Amen, the praise and the glory and the wisdom and the thanksgiving and the honour and the power and the strength is our God's unto ages of ages, Amen. 13 Then one of the elders answered, saying to me: These that are clothed in white robes, who are they and whence have they come? 14 When I said to him: My lord, thou knowest, he said to me: These are those who are coming out of the great tribulation and they have washed their robes and made them white in the blood of the Lamb. 15 Therefore they are before the throne of God, and serve Him day and night in His temple; and He who is sitting on the throne will be a tent over them. 16 No more shall they ever hunger or thirst, neither shall the sun smite on them nor any heat[4]; 17 because the Lamb, who is in the midst of the throne, shall shepherd them and lead them to fountains of waters of life; and God shall wipe away every tear from their eyes[5].

[1] Zech. vi. 5. These are the four spirits (R.V. winds) of heaven, which go forth from standing before the Lord of all the earth. [2] Dan. vii. 2. And behold the four winds of the heaven brake forth upon the great sea. xi. 4. His kingdom...shall be divided toward the four winds of heaven. [3] Eph. iv. 30. Sealed unto the day of redemption. [4] Is. xlix. 10. They shall not hunger nor thirst; neither shall the heat nor sun smite them: for he that hath mercy on them shall lead them, even by springs of water shall he guide them. [5] Is. xxv. 8. The Lord God will wipe away tears from off all faces.

§ XXI

Ch. viii. 1–5, xvi. 4–7, viii. 6–13, ix. 1–7

1 Καὶ ὅταν ἤνοιξεν τὴν σφραγῖδα τὴν ἑβδόμην, ἐγένετο σιγὴ ἐν τῷ οὐρανῷ ὡς ἡμίωρον. 2 καὶ ἴδον τοὺς ἑπτὰ ἀγγέλους οἳ ἐνώπιον τοῦ θεοῦ ἑστήκασιν, καὶ ἐδόθησαν αὐτοῖς ἑπτὰ σάλπιγγες. 3 καὶ ἄλλος ἄγγελος ἦλθεν καὶ ἐστάθη ἐπὶ τοῦ θυσιαστηρίου ἔχων λιβανωτὸν χρυσοῦν, καὶ ἐδόθη αὐτῷ θυμιάματα πολλά, ἵνα δώσει ταῖς προσευχαῖς τῶν ἁγίων πάντων ἐπὶ τὸ θυσιαστήριον τὸ χρυσοῦν τὸ ἐνώπιον τοῦ θρόνου. 4 καὶ ἀνέβη ὁ καπνὸς τῶν θυμιαμάτων ταῖς προσευχαῖς τῶν ἁγίων ἐκ χειρὸς τοῦ ἀγγέλου ἐνώπιον τοῦ θεοῦ. 5 καὶ εἴληφεν ὁ ἄγγελος τὸν λιβανωτόν, καὶ ἐγέμισεν αὐτὸν ἐκ τοῦ πυρὸς τοῦ θυσιαστηρίου καὶ ἔβαλεν εἰς τὴν γῆν· * 4 καὶ ἐγένετο αἷμα. 5 καὶ ἤκουσα τοῦ ἀγγέλου τῶν ὑδάτων λέγοντος· δίκαιος εἶ, ὁ ὢν καὶ ὁ ἦν, ὁ ὅσιος, ὅτι ταῦτα ἔκρινας, 6 ὅτι αἵματα ἁγίων καὶ προφητῶν ἐξέχεαν· καὶ αἷμα αὐτοῖς ἔδωκας πιεῖν. * 7 καὶ ἤκουσα τοῦ θυσιαστηρίου λέγοντος· ναί, κύριε ὁ θεὸς ὁ παντοκράτωρ, ἀληθιναὶ καὶ δίκαιαι αἱ κρίσεις σου. 6 Καὶ οἱ ἑπτὰ ἄγγελοι οἱ ἔχοντες τὰς * σάλπιγγας ἡτοίμασαν αὐτοὺς ἵνα σαλπίσωσιν. * 13 καὶ ἴδον, καὶ ἤκουσα ἑνὸς ἀετοῦ πετομένου ἐν μεσουρανήματι λέγοντος φωνῇ μεγάλῃ· οὐαὶ οὐαὶ οὐαὶ τοὺς κατοικοῦντας ἐπὶ τῆς γῆς ἐκ τῶν φωνῶν τῆς σάλπιγγος τῶν * ἀγγέλων τῶν μελλόντων σαλπίζειν. 1 Καὶ ὁ πέμπτος ἄγγελος ἐσάλπισεν· καὶ ἴδον ἀστέρα ἐκ τοῦ οὐρανοῦ πεπτωκότα εἰς τὴν γῆν, καὶ ἐδόθη αὐτῷ ἡ κλεὶς τοῦ φρέατος τῆς ἀβύσσου. 2 καὶ ἤνοιξεν τὸ φρέαρ τῆς ἀβύσσου· καὶ ἀνέβη καπνὸς ἐκ τοῦ φρέατος ὡς καπνὸς καμίνου μεγάλης, καὶ ἐσκοτώθη ὁ ἥλιος καὶ ὁ ἀήρ. * 3 καὶ ἐκ τοῦ καπνοῦ ἐξῆλθον ἀκρίδες εἰς τὴν γῆν, καὶ ἐδόθη αὐτοῖς ἐξουσία ὡς ἔχουσιν ἐξουσίαν οἱ σκορπίοι τῆς γῆς. 4 καὶ ἐρρέθη αὐτοῖς ἵνα μὴ ἀδικήσουσιν, * εἰ μὴ τοὺς ἀνθρώπους οἵτινες οὐκ ἔχουσιν τὴν σφραγῖδα τοῦ θεοῦ ἐπὶ τῶν μετώπων. 5 καὶ ἐδόθη αὐτοῖς ἵνα μὴ ἀποκτείνωσιν αὐτούς, ἀλλ' ἵνα βασανισθήσονται μῆνας πέντε· καὶ ὁ βασανισμὸς αὐτῶν ὡς βασανισμὸς σκορπίου, ὅταν παίσῃ ἄνθρωπον. 6 καὶ ἐν ταῖς ἡμέραις ἐκείναις ζητήσουσιν οἱ ἄνθρωποι τὸν θάνατον καὶ οὐ μὴ εὑρήσουσιν αὐτόν, καὶ ἐπιθυμήσουσιν ἀποθανεῖν καὶ φεύγει ὁ θάνατος ἀπ' αὐτῶν. 7 καὶ τὰ ὁμοιώματα τῶν

§ XXI

THE FIRST WOE

viii. 1 And when he had opened the seventh seal, silence was in heaven as it were half an hour. 2 Then I saw the seven angels who stand before God, and seven trumpets were given them. 3 Another angel then came and took his stand by the altar. He had a golden censer, and much incense was given him, that he might offer with the prayers of all the saints on the golden altar, that which is before the throne. 4 Then from the angel's hand the smoke of the incense with the prayers of the saints went up before God. 5 Then the angel took the censer and filled it from the fire of the altar and cast it on to the earth. xvi. 4 And it became blood. 5 And I heard the angel of the waters saying, Righteous art Thou O Lord, who art and who wast, the holy one, because thou hast judged these things, 6 because they have poured out the blood of saints and prophets, so thou hast given them blood to drink. 7 And I heard *the angel* of the altar saying: Yea Lord, All-sovereign God, true and righteous are Thy judgments. viii. 6 When the seven angels who had the trumpets had made themselves ready to blow, 13 I saw and heard an eagle flying in mid-air saying with a great voice: Woe, woe, woe to those who dwell on the earth from the voices of the trumpet of the angels which are about to sound[1]! ix. 1 Then the fifth angel sounded: and I saw a star fallen from the heavens to the earth; and to him was given the key of the pit of the abyss. 2 He opened the pit of the abyss; and smoke rose from the pit like the smoke of a great furnace, till the sun and the air were made dark[2]. 3 And from the smoke came forth locusts on to the earth, and such power was given them as have earthly scorpions. 4 And it was told them to hurt nothing save the men who have not the seal of God on their foreheads. 5 Even these it was charged them not to kill, but they were to be tortured five months[3], their anguish as the anguish of a scorpion when it strikes a man. 6 In those days shall men seek death and in no way find it. They shall desire to die, while death flees from them. 7 The appearances

[1] Hos. viii. 1. Set the trumpet to thy mouth. As an eagle he cometh against the house of the Lord: because they have transgressed my covenant and trespassed against my law. [2] Joel ii. 2. A day of darkness and gloominess, a day of clouds and thick darkness. *v.* 10. The sun and the moon are darkened, and the stars withdraw their shining. [3] Gen. vii. 24. And the waters prevailed upon the earth an hundred and fifty days. [4] Job iii. 21. Which long for death, but it cometh not, and dig for it more than for hid treasures.

§ XXII

Ch. ix. 7–21

ἀκρίδων ὅμοιοι ἵπποις ἡτοιμασμένοις εἰς πόλεμον, καὶ ἐπὶ τὰς κεφαλὰς αὐτῶν ὡς στέφανοι ὅμοιοι χρυσῷ, καὶ τὰ πρόσωπα αὐτῶν ὡς πρόσωπα ἀνθρώπων, 8 καὶ εἶχαν τρίχας ὡς τρίχας γυναικῶν, καὶ οἱ ὀδόντες αὐτῶν ὡς λεόντων ἦσαν, 9 καὶ εἶχον θώρακας ὡς θώρακας σιδηροῦς, καὶ ἡ φωνὴ τῶν πτερύγων αὐτῶν ὡς φωνὴ ἁρμάτων ἵππων πολλῶν τρεχόντων εἰς πόλεμον. 10 καὶ ἔχουσιν οὐρὰς ὁμοίας σκορπίοις καὶ κέντρα, καὶ ἐν ταῖς οὐραῖς αὐτῶν ἡ ἐξουσία αὐτῶν ἀδικῆσαι τοὺς ἀνθρώπους μῆνας πέντε· 11 ἔχουσιν ἐπ᾽ αὐτῶν βασιλέα τὸν ἄγγελον τῆς ἀβύσσου, ᾧ ὄνομα αὐτῷ Ἑβραϊστὶ Ἀβαδδών, καὶ ἐν τῇ Ἑλληνικῇ ὄνομα ἔχει Ἀπολλύων. 12 Ἡ οὐαὶ ἡ μία ἀπῆλθεν· ἰδοὺ ἔρχεται ἔτι δύο οὐαὶ μετὰ ταῦτα. 13 Καὶ ὁ ἕκτος ἄγγελος ἐσάλπισεν· καὶ ἤκουσα φωνὴν μίαν ἐκ τῶν τεσσάρων κεράτων τοῦ θυσιαστηρίου τοῦ χρυσοῦ τοῦ ἐνώπιον τοῦ θεοῦ, 14 λέγοντα (τοῖς τέσσαρσιν ἀγγέλοις οἱ ἔχοντες τὰς σάλπιγγας· λῦσον[1]) τοὺς δεδεμένους ἐπὶ τῷ ποταμῷ τῷ μεγάλῳ Εὐφράτῃ. 15 καὶ οἱ τέσσαρες ἄγγελοι ἐσάλπισαν καὶ ἐλύθησαν οἱ ἡτοιμασμένοι εἰς τὴν ὥραν καὶ ἡμέραν καὶ μῆνα καὶ ἐνιαυτόν, ἵνα ἀποκτείνωσιν τὸ τρίτον τῶν ἀνθρώπων. 16 καὶ ὁ ἀριθμὸς τῶν στρατευμάτων τοῦ ἱππικοῦ δισμυριάδες μυριάδων· ἤκουσα τὸν ἀριθμὸν αὐτῶν. 17 καὶ οὕτως ἴδον τοὺς ἵππους ἐν τῇ ὁράσει καὶ τοὺς καθημένους ἐπ᾽ αὐτῶν, ἔχοντας θώρακας πυρίνους καὶ ὑακινθίνους καὶ θειώδεις· καὶ αἱ κεφαλαὶ τῶν ἵππων ὡς κεφαλαὶ λεόντων, καὶ ἐκ τῶν στομάτων αὐτῶν ἐκπορεύεται πῦρ καὶ καπνὸς καὶ θεῖον. * 19 ἡ γὰρ ἐξουσία τῶν ἵππων ἐν τῷ στόματι αὐτῶν ἐστὶν καὶ ἐν ταῖς οὐραῖς αὐτῶν· αἱ γὰρ οὐραὶ αὐτῶν ὅμοιαι ὄφεσιν, ἔχουσαι κεφαλάς, καὶ ἐν αὐταῖς ἀδικοῦσιν. 20 καὶ οἱ λοιποὶ τῶν ἀνθρώπων, οἳ οὐκ ἀπεκτάνθησαν ἐν ταῖς πληγαῖς ταύταις, οὐδὲ μετενόησαν ἐκ τῶν ἔργων τῶν χειρῶν αὐτῶν, ἵνα μὴ προσκυνήσουσιν τὰ δαιμόνια καὶ τὰ εἴδωλα τὰ χρυσᾶ καὶ τὰ ἀργυρᾶ καὶ τὰ χαλκᾶ καὶ τὰ λίθινα καὶ τὰ ξύλινα, ἃ οὔτε βλέπειν δύνανται οὔτε ἀκούειν οὔτε περιπατεῖν, 21 καὶ οὐ μετενόησαν ἐκ τῶν φόνων αὐτῶν οὔτε ἐκ τῶν φαρμακιῶν αὐτῶν οὔτε ἐκ τῆς πορνείας αὐτῶν οὔτε ἐκ τῶν κλεμμάτων αὐτῶν.

[1] Text: τῷ ἕκτῳ ἀγγέλῳ, ὁ ἔχων τὴν σάλπιγγα· λῦσον τοὺς τέσσαρας ἀγγέλους.

§ XXII

THE SECOND WOE

ix. 7 of the locusts were like horses made ready for battle[1], and on their heads as it were crowns resembling gold, and their faces as human faces, 8 and they had hair as women's hair, and their teeth were as those of lions. 9 Breastplates they had like iron breastplates, and the noise of their wings was as the noise of many horse-chariots racing into battle[2]. 10 They have tails like scorpions and stings. In their tails is their power to hurt men five months[3]. 11 Over them they have as king the angel of the abyss, whose name in Hebrew is Abaddon and in the Greek he has the name Apollyon. 12 The first woe is past. Lo, there come yet two woes after. 13 Then the sixth angel sounded; and I heard one blast from the four horns of the altar of gold[4] that is before God, 14 saying to the four angels—those having the trumpets—Set free those who are bound at the river, the Great Euphrates. 15 Then the four angels blew: and there were set free those who had been made ready for this hour and day and month and year, that they might kill one third of men. 16 The number of the armies of cavalry was twice a myriad myriad. I heard their number, 17 and I saw how the horses and those sitting on them were in appearance, having breastplates fiery and dark-red and sulphurous. And the heads of their horses as lions' heads, and from their mouths go out fire, smoke and brimstone. 19 For the power of the horses is in their mouth and in their tails; for their tails are like serpents, having heads, and with them they injure[5]. 20 Yet the rest of the men, who were not slain by these plagues, neither repented of the works of their hands, that they should not worship the demons and the idols of gold, silver, brass, stone or wood, which cannot see or hear or walk, 21 nor did they repent of their murders or of their sorceries or of their fornication or of their thefts.

[1] Joel ii. 4. The appearance of them is as the appearance of horses; and as horsemen do they run. [2] Joel ii. 5. Like the noise of chariots on the tops of the mountains. [3] Is. xxx. 6. Through the land of trouble and anguish, from whence come the lioness and the lion, the viper and fiery flying serpent. [4] Ex. xxvii. 2. The horns of it upon the four corners thereof. [5] Prov. xxiii. 32. Read as: the end biteth like a serpent and stingeth like an adder.

§ XXIII

CH. xi. 14–19, xiv. 1–5, 13–14

14 Ἡ οὐαὶ ἡ δευτέρα ἀπῆλθεν· ἰδοὺ ἡ οὐαὶ ἡ τρίτη ἔρχεται ταχύ. 15 Καὶ ὁ ἕβδομος ἄγγελος ἐσάλπισεν· καὶ ἐγένοντο φωναὶ μεγάλαι ἐν τῷ οὐρανῷ, λέγοντες· ἐγένετο ἡ βασιλεία τοῦ κόσμου τοῦ κυρίου ἡμῶν καὶ τοῦ Χριστοῦ αὐτοῦ, καὶ βασιλεύσει εἰς τοὺς αἰῶνας τῶν αἰώνων. 16 καὶ οἱ εἴκοσι τέσσαρες πρεσβύτεροι οἱ ἐνώπιον τοῦ θεοῦ, οἳ κάθηνται ἐπὶ τοὺς θρόνους αὐτῶν, ἔπεσαν ἐπὶ τὰ πρόσωπα αὐτῶν καὶ προσεκύνησαν τῷ θεῷ, 17 λέγοντες· εὐχαριστοῦμέν σοι, κύριε ὁ θεὸς ὁ παντοκράτωρ, ὁ ὢν καὶ ὁ ἦν, καὶ ὅτι εἴληφας τὴν δύναμίν σου τὴν μεγάλην καὶ ἐβασίλευσας, 18 καὶ τὰ ἔθνη ὠργίσθησαν, καὶ ἦλθεν ἡ ὀργή σου καὶ ὁ καιρὸς τῶν νεκρῶν κριθῆναι καὶ δοῦναι τὸν μισθὸν τοῖς δούλοις σου τοῖς προφήταις καὶ τοῖς ἁγίοις καὶ τοῖς φοβουμένοις τὸ ὄνομά σου, * καὶ διαφθεῖραι τοὺς διαφθείροντας τὴν γῆν. 19 καὶ ἠνοίγη ὁ ναὸς τοῦ θεοῦ ὁ ἐν τῷ οὐρανῷ, καὶ ὤφθη ἡ κιβωτὸς τῆς διαθήκης αὐτοῦ ἐν τῷ ναῷ αὐτοῦ. 1 καὶ ἴδον, καὶ ἰδοὺ τὸ ἀρνίον ἑστὸς ἐπὶ τὸ ὄρος Σιών, καὶ μετ' αὐτοῦ ἑκατὸν τεσσεράκοντα τέσσαρες χιλιάδες ἔχουσαι τὸ ὄνομα αὐτοῦ καὶ τὸ ὄνομα τοῦ πατρὸς αὐτοῦ γεγραμμένον ἐπὶ τῶν μετώπων αὐτῶν. 2 καὶ ἤκουσα φωνὴν ἐκ τοῦ οὐρανοῦ ὡς φωνὴν ὑδάτων πολλῶν καὶ ὡς φωνὴν βροντῆς μεγάλης, καὶ ἡ φωνὴ ἣν ἤκουσα ὡς κιθαρῳδῶν κιθαριζόντων ἐν ταῖς κιθάραις αὐτῶν· 3 καὶ ᾄδουσιν ᾠδὴν καινὴν ἐνώπιον τοῦ θρόνου καὶ ἐνώπιον τῶν τεσσάρων ζώων καὶ τῶν πρεσβυτέρων· καὶ οὐδεὶς ἐδύνατο μαθεῖν τὴν ᾠδὴν εἰ μὴ αἱ ἑκατὸν τεσσεράκοντα τέσσαρες χιλιάδες, οἱ ἠγορασμένοι ἀπὸ τῆς γῆς. 4 οὗτοί εἰσιν οἳ μετὰ γυναικῶν οὐκ ἐμολύνθησαν, παρθένοι γάρ εἰσιν οὗτοι οἱ ἀκολουθοῦντες τῷ ἀρνίῳ ὅπου ἂν ὑπάγῃ. οὗτοι ἠγοράσθησαν ἀπὸ τῶν ἀνθρώπων ἀπαρχὴ τῷ θεῷ καὶ τῷ ἀρνίῳ, 5 καὶ ἐν τῷ στόματι αὐτῶν οὐχ εὑρέθη ψεῦδος· ἄμωμοι γάρ εἰσιν. 13 καὶ ἤκουσα φωνῆς ἐκ τοῦ οὐρανοῦ λεγούσης· γράψον· μακάριοι οἱ νεκροὶ οἱ ἐν κυρίῳ ἀποθνήσκοντες ἀπάρτι. ναί, λέγει τὸ πνεῦμα, ἵνα ἀναπαήσονται ἐκ τῶν κόπων αὐτῶν· τὰ γὰρ ἔργα αὐτῶν ἀκολουθεῖ μετ' αὐτῶν. 14 Καὶ ἴδον, καὶ ἰδοὺ νεφέλη λευκή, καὶ ἐπὶ τὴν νεφέλην καθήμενον ὅμοιον υἱὸν ἀνθρώπου, ἔχων

§ XXIII

The Third Woe

xi. 14 The second woe has passed. Lo the third woe comes quickly. 15 Then the seventh angel sounded; and there were great voices in heaven saying: The kingdom of the world has become our Lord's and His Christ's, and He shall reign unto ages of ages. 16 Then the twenty-four elders who are before God, who were seated on their thrones, fell on their faces and made obeisance to God, 17 saying: We render thanks to Thee, O Lord the All-sovereign God, who art and who wast, because Thou hast taken Thy great power and reigned. 18 The nations raged, but Thy wrath has come, and it is the time for the dead to be judged and to give the reward to Thy servants the prophets and the saints and those that fear Thy name, and to destroy those who destroy the earth[1]. 19 Then the temple of God which is in heaven was opened, and the ark of His covenant was seen in His temple[2]. xiv. 1 Then I beheld and lo the Lamb standing on Mount Zion, and with him a hundred and forty-four thousand having His name and the name of His Father written on their foreheads[3]. 2 And I heard a sound from heaven as a sound of many waters, as a sound of great thunder. The sound which I heard was as of harpers harping with their harps. 3 And they sing a new song before the Throne and before the four living creatures and the elders. And no one could learn the song save the hundred and forty and four thousand, the redeemed from the earth. 4 These are they who have not been defiled with women, for they are virgins, those following the Lamb wherever he may go. These have been redeemed from among men, first-fruits to God and to the Lamb, 5 and in whose mouth is found no guile, for they are blameless[4]. 13 Then I heard a voice from heaven saying: Write, Blessed are the dead who die in the Lord from henceforth. Yea, says the Spirit, seeing they shall rest from their labours[5]. For their works follow with them. 14 Then I saw, and lo a white cloud, and sitting on the cloud was one like a son of man[6], having

[1] Dan. ix. 27. Until the determined consummation is poured out on the desolator.
[2] 1 K. viii. 21. The ark, wherein is the covenant of the Lord. [3] Is. xiv. 22. The Lord hath founded Zion, and in her shall the afflicted of his people take refuge. (This connects the 144,000 with the holy remnant.) [4] Is. liii. 9. Although he had done no violence, neither was any deceit in his mouth. (Last transferred to saints.)
[5] Many O.T. passages. Heb. iv. 9. There remaineth therefore a Sabbath rest for the people of God. [6] Lk. xxi. 27. See the Son of Man coming in a cloud with power and great glory.

§ XXIV

Ch. xiv. 14–19, xv. 1, xv. 6–xvi. 1, xv. 2–4

ἐπὶ τῆς κεφαλῆς αὐτοῦ στέφανον χρυσοῦν καὶ ἐν τῇ χειρὶ αὐτοῦ δρέπανον ὀξύ. 15 καὶ ἄλλος ἄγγελος ἐξῆλθεν ἐκ τοῦ ναοῦ, κράζων ἐν φωνῇ μεγάλῃ τῷ καθημένῳ ἐπὶ τῆς νεφέλης· πέμψον τὸ δρέπανόν σου καὶ θέρισον, ὅτι ἦλθεν ἡ ὥρα θερίσαι, ὅτι ἐξηράνθη ὁ θερισμὸς τῆς γῆς. 16 καὶ ἔβαλεν ὁ καθήμενος ἐπὶ τῆς νεφέλης τὸ δρέπανον αὐτοῦ ἐπὶ τὴν γῆν, καὶ ἐθερίσθη ἡ γῆ. 17 καὶ ἄλλος ἄγγελος ἐξῆλθεν ἐκ τοῦ ναοῦ τοῦ ἐν τῷ οὐρανῷ, ἔχων καὶ αὐτὸς δρέπανον ὀξύ· 18 καὶ ἄλλος ἄγγελος ἐξῆλθεν ἐκ τοῦ θυσιαστηρίου, ἔχων ἐξουσίαν ἐπὶ τοῦ πυρός, καὶ ἐφώνησεν φωνῇ μεγάλῃ τῷ ἔχοντι τὸ δρέπανον τὸ ὀξὺ λέγων· πέμψον σου τὸ δρέπανον τὸ ὀξὺ καὶ τρύγησον τοὺς βότρυας τῆς ἀμπέλου τῆς γῆς, ὅτι ἤκμασαν αἱ σταφυλαὶ αὐτῆς. 19 καὶ ἔβαλεν ὁ ἄγγελος τὸ δρέπανον αὐτοῦ εἰς τὴν γῆν, καὶ ἐτρύγησεν τὴν ἄμπελον τῆς γῆς. * 1 Καὶ ἴδον ἄλλο σημεῖον ἐν τῷ οὐρανῷ μέγα καὶ θαυμαστόν, ἀγγέλους ἑπτὰ ἔχοντας πληγὰς ἑπτὰ τὰς ἐσχάτας, ὅτι ἐν αὐταῖς ἐτελέσθη ὁ θυμὸς τοῦ θεοῦ, 6 καὶ περιεζωσμένοι περὶ τὰ στήθη ζώνας χρυσᾶς. 7 καὶ ἓν ἐκ τῶν τεσσάρων ζώων ἔδωκεν τοῖς ἑπτὰ ἀγγέλοις ἑπτὰ φιάλας χρυσᾶς γεμούσας τοῦ θυμοῦ τοῦ θεοῦ τοῦ ζῶντος εἰς τοὺς αἰῶνας τῶν αἰώνων. 8 καὶ ἐγεμίσθη ὁ ναὸς καπνοῦ ἐκ τῆς δόξης τοῦ θεοῦ καὶ ἐκ τῆς δυνάμεως αὐτοῦ. καὶ οὐδεὶς ἐδύνατο εἰσελθεῖν εἰς τὸν ναὸν ἄχρι τελεσθῶσιν αἱ ἑπτὰ πληγαὶ τῶν ἑπτὰ ἀγγέλων. 1 καὶ ἤκουσα μεγάλης φωνῆς ἐκ τοῦ ναοῦ λεγούσης τοῖς ἑπτὰ ἀγγέλοις· ὑπάγετε καὶ ἐκχέετε τὰς ἑπτὰ φιάλας τοῦ θυμοῦ τοῦ θεοῦ εἰς τὴν γῆν. 2 καὶ ἴδον ὡς θάλασσαν ὑαλίνην μεμιγμένην πυρί, καὶ τοὺς νικῶντας ἐκ τοῦ θηρίου καὶ ἐκ τῆς εἰκόνος αὐτοῦ καὶ ἐκ τοῦ ἀριθμοῦ τοῦ ὀνόματος αὐτοῦ ἑστῶτας ἐπὶ τὴν θάλασσαν τὴν ὑαλίνην, ἔχοντας κιθάρας τοῦ θεοῦ. 3 καὶ ᾄδουσιν τὴν ᾠδὴν Μωϋσέως τοῦ δούλου τοῦ θεοῦ καὶ τὴν ᾠδὴν τοῦ ἀρνίου, λέγοντες· *μεγάλα καὶ θαυμαστὰ τὰ ἔργα σου, κύριε ὁ θεὸς ὁ παντοκράτωρ· δίκαιαι καὶ ἀληθιναὶ αἱ ὁδοί σου, ὁ βασιλεὺς τῶν ἐθνῶν·* 4 *τίς οὐ μὴ φοβηθῇ*, κύριε, καὶ *δοξάσει τὸ ὄνομά σου;* ὅτι μόνος *ὅσιος*, ὅτι *πάντα τὰ ἔθνη ἥξουσιν καὶ προσκυνήσουσιν ἐνώπιόν σου*, ὅτι τὰ δικαιώματά σου ἐφανερώθησαν.

§ XXIV

Ingathering of Good and Destruction of Evil

xiv. 14 on his head a golden coronet and in his hand a sharp sickle. 15 Then another angel came out from the temple crying with a great voice to him sitting on the cloud: Put forth thy sickle and reap, for the hour has come to reap, for the harvest of the world is over-ripe[1]. 16 Then he who sat on the cloud put his sickle to the earth, and the earth was reaped. 17 Then another angel came out from the temple which is in heaven, he too having a sharp sickle. 18 And another angel came out from the altar—the one who had the charge of the fire. With a great voice he called to him who had the sharp sickle, saying: Put forth thy sharp sickle and gather the clusters of the vine of the earth, for its grapes are just ripe. 19 Then the angel put his sickle to the earth and gathered the vine of the earth. xv. 1 Then I saw another sign in heaven, great and wonderful, seven angels having seven plagues, the last, for by them is brought to completion the anger of God, 6 and they were girt about the breasts with golden girdles. 7 Then one of the four living creatures gave to the seven angels seven golden vials full of the wrath of God, the living one unto ages of ages. 8 Then was the temple filled with smoke from God's glory and His might. And no one could enter into the temple until the seven plagues of the seven angels were finished. xvi. 1 Then I heard a great voice from the temple saying to the seven angels: Go and pour out the seven vials of God's wrath on the earth. xv. 2 And I saw, as it were a glassy sea mingled with fire, and those who had come victorious from the beast and his image and the number of his name, standing by the glassy sea, having harps of God. 3 They sing the song of Moses the servant of God, and the song of the Lamb, saying: Great and wonderful are Thy works, O Lord, All-sovereign God. Righteous and true are Thy ways, O king of the nations. 4 Who would not fear Thee, O Lord, and glorify Thy name? Because Thou only art holy, for all the nations shall come and worship before Thee, for Thy righteous doings have been made manifest.

[1] Mk iv. 29. But when the fruit is ripe, straightway he putteth forth the sickle, because the harvest is come.

§ XXV

Ch. xxi. 9–24

9 Καὶ ἦλθεν εἷς ἐκ τῶν ἑπτὰ ἀγγέλων τῶν ἐχόντων τὰς ἑπτὰ φιάλας τῶν γεμόντων τῶν ἑπτὰ πληγῶν τῶν ἐσχάτων, καὶ ἐλάλησεν μετ' ἐμοῦ λέγων· δεῦρο, δείξω σοι τὴν νύμφην τὴν γυναῖκα τοῦ ἀρνίου. 10 καὶ ἀπήνεγκέν με ἐν πνεύματι ἐπὶ ὄρος μέγα καὶ ὑψηλόν, καὶ ἔδειξέν μοι τὴν πόλιν τὴν ἁγίαν Ἱερουσαλὴμ καταβαίνουσαν ἐκ τοῦ οὐρανοῦ ἀπὸ τοῦ θεοῦ, (ἡτοιμασμένην ὡς νύμφην κεκοσμημένην τῷ ανδρὶ αὐτῆς,) 11 ἔχουσαν τὴν δόξαν τοῦ θεοῦ· ὁ φωστὴρ αὐτῆς ὅμοιος λίθῳ τιμιωτάτῳ, ὡς λίθῳ ἰάσπιδι κρυσταλλίζοντι· 12 ἔχουσα τεῖχος μέγα καὶ ὑψηλόν, ἔχουσα πυλῶνας δώδεκα, καὶ ἐπὶ τοῖς πυλῶσιν ἀγγέλους δώδεκα, καὶ ὀνόματα ἐπιγεγραμμένα, ἅ ἐστιν τῶν δώδεκα φυλῶν υἱῶν Ἰσραήλ. 13 ἀπὸ ἀνατολῆς πυλῶνες τρεῖς, καὶ ἀπὸ βορρᾶ πυλῶνες τρεῖς, καὶ ἀπὸ νότου πυλῶνες τρεῖς, καὶ ἀπὸ δυσμῶν πυλῶνες τρεῖς. 14 καὶ τὸ τεῖχος τῆς πόλεως ἔχων θεμελίους δώδεκα, καὶ ἐπ' αὐτῶν δώδεκα ὀνόματα τῶν δώδεκα ἀποστόλων τοῦ ἀρνίου. 15 καὶ ὁ λαλῶν μετ' ἐμοῦ εἶχεν μέτρον κάλαμον χρυσοῦν, ἵνα μετρήσῃ τὴν πόλιν καὶ τοὺς πυλῶνας αὐτῆς καὶ τὸ τεῖχος αὐτῆς. 16 καὶ ἡ πόλις τετράγωνος κεῖται, καὶ τὸ μῆκος αὐτῆς ὅσον τὸ πλάτος. καὶ ἐμέτρησεν τὴν πόλιν τῷ καλάμῳ ἐπὶ σταδίων δώδεκα χιλιάδων· τὸ μῆκος καὶ τὸ πλάτος καὶ τὸ ὕψος αὐτῆς ἴσα ἐστίν. 17 καὶ ἐμέτρησεν τὸ τεῖχος αὐτῆς ἑκατὸν τεσσεράκοντα τεσσάρων πηχῶν, μέτρον ἀνθρώπου, ὅ ἐστιν ἀγγέλου. 18 καὶ ἡ ἐνδώμησις τοῦ τείχους αὐτῆς ἴασπις, καὶ ἡ πόλις χρυσίον καθαρὸν ὅμοιον ὑάλῳ καθαρῷ. 19 οἱ θεμέλιοι τοῦ τείχους τῆς πόλεως παντὶ λίθῳ τιμίῳ κεκοσμημένοι· ἴασπις, σάπφειρος, χαλκηδών, σμάραγδος, 20 σαρδόνυξ, σάρδιον, χρυσόλιθος, βήρυλλος, τοπάζιον, χρυσόπρασος, ὑάκινθος, ἀμέθυστος. 21 καὶ οἱ δώδεκα πυλῶνες δώδεκα μαργαρῖται· ἀνὰ εἷς ἕκαστος τῶν πυλώνων ἦν ἐξ ἑνὸς μαργαρίτου. καὶ ἡ πλατεῖα τῆς πόλεως χρυσίον καθαρὸν ὡς ὕαλος διαυγής. 22 καὶ ναὸν οὐκ εἶδον ἐν αὐτῇ· ὁ γὰρ κύριος ὁ θεὸς ὁ παντοκράτωρ ναὸς αὐτῆς ἐστίν, καὶ τὸ ἀρνίον. 23 καὶ ἡ πόλις οὐ χρείαν ἔχει τοῦ ἡλίου οὐδὲ τοῦ λύχνου, ἵνα φαίνωσιν αὐτῇ· ἡ γὰρ δόξα τοῦ θεοῦ ἐφώτισεν αὐτήν, 24 καὶ περιπατήσουσιν τὰ ἔθνη

§ XXV

The Holy Jerusalem

xxi. 9 Then came to me one of the seven angels who had the seven vials full of the seven last plagues and spake with me saying: Come, I will show thee the bride, the Lamb's wife. 10 Then he carried me in the spirit to a mountain, great and high, and showed me the city, the Holy Jerusalem, coming down out of heaven from God, prepared as a bride adorned for her husband, 11 having the glory of God. Her light was like a most precious stone, as a jasper stone clear as crystal[1]. 12 She had a wall great and high. Her gates were twelve and at the gates twelve angels[2]. And names were inscribed on them, those of the twelve tribes of the children of Israel. 13 Three gates were on the east, three on the north, three on the south and three on the west. 14 The wall of the city had twelve foundations, and on them were the twelve names of the twelve apostles of the Lamb[3]. 15 He who spake with me had, as a measure, a golden reed, that he might measure the city, her gates and her wall. 16 The city lies four-square, the length of it the same as the breadth. And he measured the city with the reed, twelve thousand furlongs—the length and the breadth and the height of it are equal. 17 Then he measured her wall, a hundred and forty-four cubits—man's measure, which is *also* angel's. 18 The material of her wall was jasper, and the city herself pure gold, like pure glass. 19 The foundations of the wall of the city were embellished with every kind of precious stone—jasper, sapphire, chalcedony, emerald, 20 sardonyx, sardius, chrysolite, beryl, topaz, chrysoprase, jacinth, amethyst. 21 The twelve gates were twelve pearls, each gate of one pearl. The street of the city was pure gold like transparent glass[4]. 22 Temple in her I saw none, for the Lord, the All-sovereign God is her temple, and the Lamb. 23 Nor has the city need of the sun or of the lamp to shine for her, because the glory of God[1] has illumined her. 24 In her light shall the nations

[1] Num. xiv. 21. And as all the earth shall be filled with the glory of the Lord. Is. lx. 18–21. Violence shall no more be heard in thy land, desolation nor destruction within thy borders; but thou shalt call thy walls Salvation and thy gates Praise. The sun shall be no more thy light by day; neither for brightness shall the moon give light unto thee; but the Lord shall be unto thee an everlasting light, and thy God thy glory. Thy sun shall no more go down, nor shall thy moon withdraw itself; for the Lord shall be thine everlasting light, and the days of thy mourning shall be ended. Thy people also shall be all righteous. [2] lxii. 6. I have set watchmen upon thy walls, O Jerusalem. [3] Ex. xxviii. 30. The gates after the names of the tribes of Israel on the breastplate. [4] Is. liv. 11, 12, 14. I will set thy stones in fair colours and lay thy foundations with sapphires...and all thy border of pleasant stones....In righteousness shalt thou be established. Is. lx. 17. For brass I will bring gold.

§ XXVI

CH. xxi. 24—xxii. 5, 6, 8, 9, xvi. 15, xxii. 14–17, 20[1]

διὰ τοῦ φωτὸς αὐτῆς, καὶ οἱ βασιλεῖς τῆς γῆς, * 25 καὶ οἱ πυλῶνες αὐτῆς οὐ μὴ κλεισθῶσιν ἡμέρας, νὺξ γὰρ οὐκ ἔσται ἐκεῖ, 26 καὶ οἴσουσιν τὴν δόξαν καὶ τὴν τιμὴν τῶν ἐθνῶν εἰς αὐτήν. 27 καὶ οὐ μὴ εἰσέλθῃ εἰς αὐτὴν πᾶν κοινὸν καὶ ὁ ποιῶν βδέλυγμα καὶ ψεῦδος. * 1 Και ἔδειξέν μοι ποταμὸν ὕδατος ζωῆς λαμπρὸν ὡς κρύσταλλον, ἐκπορευόμενον ἐκ τοῦ θρόνου τοῦ θεοῦ. * 2 ἐν μέσῳ τῆς πλατείας αὐτῆς καὶ τοῦ ποταμοῦ ἐντεῦθεν καὶ ἐκεῖθεν ξύλον ζωῆς ποιῶν καρποὺς δώδεκα, κατὰ μῆνα ἕκαστον ἀποδιδοὺς τὸν καρπὸν αὐτοῦ, καὶ τὰ φύλλα τοῦ ξύλου εἰς θεραπείαν τῶν ἐθνῶν. 3 καὶ πᾶν κατάθεμα οὐκ ἔσται ἔτι. καὶ ὁ θρόνος * τοῦ ἀρνίου ἐν αὐτῇ ἔσται, καὶ οἱ δοῦλοι αὐτοῦ λατρεύσουσιν αὐτῷ 4 καὶ ὄψονται τὸ πρόσωπον αὐτοῦ, καὶ τὸ ὄνομα αὐτοῦ ἐπὶ τῶν μετώπων αὐτῶν. 5 * καὶ οὐκ ἔχουσιν χρείαν φωτὸς λύχνου καὶ φωτὸς ἡλίου· ὅτι κύριος ὁ θεὸς φωτιεῖ ἐπ' αὐτούς, * (καὶ ὁ λύχνος αὐτῶν τὸ ἀρνίον). 6 καὶ εἶπέν μοι· οὗτοι οἱ λόγοι πιστοὶ καὶ ἀληθινοί, καὶ ὁ κύριος ὁ θεὸς τῶν πνευμάτων τῶν προφητῶν ἀπέστειλεν τὸν ἄγγελον αὐτοῦ δεῖξαι τοῖς δούλοις αὐτοῦ ἃ δεῖ γενέσθαι ἐν τάχει. 8 κἀγὼ Ἰωάννης ὁ βλέπων καὶ ἀκούων ταῦτα· καὶ ὅτε ἤκουσα καὶ ἔβλεψα, ἔπεσα προσκυνῆσαι ἔμπροσθεν τῶν ποδῶν τοῦ ἀγγέλου τοῦ δεικνύντος μοι ταῦτα. 9 καὶ λέγει μοι· ὅρα μή· σύνδουλός σου εἰμὶ καὶ τῶν ἀδελφῶν σου τῶν προφητῶν (καὶ τῶν ἐχόντων τὴν μαρτυρίαν Ἰησοῦ). τῷ θεῷ προσκύνησον. (ἡ γὰρ μαρτυρία Ἰησοῦ) ἐστὶν τὸ πνεῦμα τῆς προφητείας. * (15 ἰδοὺ ἔρχομαι ὡς κλέπτης· μακάριος ὁ γρηγορῶν καὶ τηρῶν τὰ ἱμάτια αὐτοῦ, μὴ γυμνὸς περιπατῇ καὶ βλέπωσιν τὴν ἀσχημοσύνην αὐτοῦ.) 14 μακάριοι οἱ πλύνοντες τὰς στολὰς αὐτῶν, ἵνα ἔσται ἡ ἐξουσία αὐτῶν ἐπὶ τὸ ξύλον τῆς ζωῆς καὶ τοῖς πυλῶσιν εἰσέλθωσιν εἰς τὴν πόλιν. 15 ἔξω οἱ κύνες καὶ οἱ φαρμακοὶ καὶ οἱ πόρνοι καὶ οἱ φονεῖς καὶ οἱ εἰδωλολάτραι καὶ πᾶς ποιῶν καὶ φιλῶν ψεῦδος. 16 ἐγὼ Ἰησοῦς ἔπεμψα τὸν ἄγγελόν μου μαρτυρῆσαι ὑμῖν ταῦτα ἐπὶ ταῖς ἐκκλησίαις. ἐγώ εἰμι ἡ ῥίζα καὶ τὸ γένος Δαυείδ, ὁ ἀστὴρ ὁ λαμπρὸς ὁ πρωϊνός. 17 καὶ τὸ πνεῦμα καὶ ἡ νύμφη λέγουσιν· ἔρχου. καὶ ὁ ἀκούων εἰπάτω· ἔρχου. 20 Λέγει ὁ μαρτυρῶν ταῦτα· * Ἀμήν, ἔρχου κύριε Ἰησοῦ.

[1] Passages in brackets from xix. 10.

§ XXVI

THE HOLY JERUSALEM

xxi. 24 and the kings of the earth walk. 25 Her gates shall not be shut by day, for night is not there. 26 And they will bring into her the glory and the honour of the nations[1]. 27 Nothing profane shall enter her, no one doing abomination or falsehood. xxii. 1 Then he showed me a river of water of life, bright like crystal, issuing forth from the throne of God. 2 In the middle of her street and on both sides of the river was a tree of life, bearing twelve fruitings, producing its fruit each month. And the leaves of the tree are for the healing of the nations[2]. 3 Nothing dedicated to evil shall be any more, but the throne of the Lamb shall be in her, and His servants shall serve Him 4 and shall see His face, having His name on their foreheads. 5 And they have no need of light of lamp or light of sun because the Lord God shall shine on them and the Lamb is their lamp[3]. 6 And he said to me: These words are faithful and true, and the Lord, the God of the spirits of the prophets, has sent his angel to show to his servants what must come to pass shortly. 8 And I John am he who saw and heard these things. And when I had seen and heard, I fell to worship before the feet of the angel who showed me these things. 9 And he says to me: See not to. I am thy fellow-servant and of thy brethren the prophets and of those who have the witness of Jesus. Worship God. For the witness of Jesus is the spirit of prophecy. xvi. 15 Lo I come as a thief. Blessed is he who is watching and keeping his garments clean[4] that he walk not naked and men see his shame. xxii. 14 Blessed are those who are washing their robes, that their authority may be over the tree of life when they have entered by the gates into the city. 15 Without are the shameless, the sorcerers, the fornicators, the murderers, the idolaters, and everyone making and loving falsehood. 16 I Jesus have sent my angel to testify to you these things concerning the churches. I am the root and the descendant of David, the bright morning star. 17 The Spirit and the bride say, come. And whosoever hears let him say, come. 20 And he who witnesses these things says: Yea, Amen, come Lord Jesus.

[1] Is. lx. 11. Thy gates shall be open continually; they shall not be shut day nor night; that men may bring unto thee the wealth of the nations, and their kings led with them. [2] Jer. ii. 13. They have forsaken me the fountain of living waters. Ez. xlvii. 12. And by the river upon the bank thereof, on this side and on that side, shall grow every tree for food, whose leaf shall not wither, neither shall the fruit thereof fail; it shall bring forth new fruit every month, because the waters thereof issue out of the sanctuary: and the fruit thereof shall be for food, and the leaf thereof for healing. [3] Is. lx. 20. Thy sun shall no more go down...for the Lord shall be thine everlasting light. [4] Lk. xii. 39, 40. If the master of the house had known in what hour the thief was coming, he would have watched....Be ye also ready, for in an hour that ye think not the Son of Man cometh.

§ XXVII

Ch. i. 3–6, xx. 1–10

3 μακάριος ὁ ἀναγινώσκων καὶ οἱ ἀκούοντες τὸν λόγον τῆς προφητείας καὶ τηροῦντες τὰ ἐν αὐτῇ γεγραμμένα· ὁ γὰρ καιρὸς ἐγγύς. 4 χάρις ὑμῖν καὶ εἰρήνη 5 ἀπὸ Ἰησοῦ Χριστοῦ, ὁ μάρτυς ὁ πιστός, ὁ πρωτότοκος τῶν νεκρῶν καὶ ὁ ἄρχων τῶν βασιλέων τῆς γῆς, τῷ ἀγαπῶντι ἡμᾶς καὶ λύσαντι ἡμᾶς ἐκ τῶν ἁμαρτιῶν ἡμῶν ἐν τῷ αἵματι αὐτοῦ. 6 καὶ ἐποίησεν ἡμᾶς βασιλείαν, ἱερεῖς τῷ θεῷ καὶ πατρὶ αὐτοῦ, αὐτῷ ἡ δόξα καὶ τὸ κράτος εἰς τοὺς αἰῶνας τῶν αἰώνων· ἀμήν. xx. 1 καὶ ἴδον ἄγγελον καταβαίνοντα ἐκ τοῦ οὐρανοῦ, ἔχοντα τὴν κλεῖν τῆς ἀβύσσου καὶ ἅλυσιν μεγάλην ἐπὶ τὴν χεῖρα αὐτοῦ. 2 καὶ ἐκράτησεν τὸν δράκοντα, ὁ ὄφις ὁ ἀρχαῖος, ὅ ἐστιν ὁ διάβολος καὶ ὁ σατανᾶς, καὶ ἔδησεν αὐτὸν χίλια ἔτη, 3 καὶ ἔβαλεν αὐτὸν εἰς τὴν ἄβυσσον, καὶ ἔκλεισεν καὶ ἐσφράγισεν ἐπάνω αὐτοῦ, ἵνα μὴ πλανήσῃ ἔτι τὰ ἔθνη, ἄχρι τελεσθῇ τὰ χίλια ἔτη· μετὰ ταῦτα δεῖ αὐτὸν λυθῆναι μικρὸν χρόνον. 4 καὶ ἴδον θρόνους, καὶ ἐκάθισαν ἐπ' αὐτούς, καὶ κρίμα ἐδόθη αὐτοῖς, καὶ τὰς ψυχὰς τῶν πεπελεκισμένων διὰ τὴν μαρτυρίαν Ἰησοῦ καὶ διὰ τὸν λόγον τοῦ θεοῦ, καὶ οἵτινες οὐ προσεκύνησαν τὸ θηρίον οὐδὲ τὴν εἰκόνα αὐτοῦ καὶ οὐκ ἔλαβον τὸ χάραγμα ἐπὶ τὸ μέτωπον καὶ ἐπὶ τὴν χεῖρα αὐτῶν· καὶ ἔζησαν καὶ ἐβασίλευσαν μετὰ τοῦ Χριστοῦ χίλια ἔτη. * 5 οἱ λοιποὶ τῶν νεκρῶν οὐκ ἔζησαν ἄχρι τελεσθῇ τὰ χίλια ἔτη. 6 μακάριος καὶ ἅγιος ὁ ἔχων μέρος ἐν τῇ ἀναστάσει τῇ πρώτῃ· ἐπὶ τούτων ὁ δεύτερος θάνατος οὐκ ἔχει ἐξουσίαν, ἀλλὰ ἔσονται ἱερεῖς τοῦ θεοῦ καὶ τοῦ Χριστοῦ, καὶ βασιλεύσουσιν μετ' αὐτοῦ τὰ χίλια ἔτη. 7 καὶ ὅταν τελεσθῇ τὰ χίλια ἔτη, λυθήσεται ὁ σατανᾶς ἐκ τῆς φυλακῆς αὐτοῦ, 8 καὶ ἐξελεύσεται πλανῆσαι τὰ ἔθνη τὰ ἐν ταῖς τέσσαρσιν γωνίαις τῆς γῆς, τὸν Γὼγ καὶ Μαγώγ, συναγαγεῖν αὐτοὺς εἰς τὸν πόλεμον, ὧν ὁ ἀριθμὸς αὐτῶν ὡς ἡ ἄμμος τῆς θαλάσσης. 9 καὶ ἀνέβησαν ἐπὶ τὸ πλάτος τῆς γῆς, καὶ ἐκύκλευσαν τὴν παρεμβολὴν τῶν ἁγίων καὶ τὴν πόλιν τὴν ἠγαπημένην· καὶ κατέβη πῦρ ἐκ τοῦ οὐρανοῦ καὶ κατέφαγεν αὐτούς· 10 καὶ ὁ διάβολος ὁ πλανῶν αὐτοὺς ἐβλήθη εἰς τὴν λίμνην τοῦ πυρὸς καὶ τοῦ θείου, ὅπου καὶ τὸ θηρίον καὶ ὁ ψευδοπροφήτης. *

§ XXVII

i. 3 Blessed is he who reads and those who hear the word of the prophecy and hold fast the things written in it. For the time is near. 4 Grace to you and peace 5 from Jesus Christ, the faithful witness, the firstborn of the dead and the ruler of the kings of the earth. To Him who loves us and has loosed us from our sins by His blood, 6 and made us a kingdom, priests to God, even His Father, to Him be the glory and the power for ever and ever. Amen. xx. 1 Then I saw an angel coming down out of heaven, having the key of the abyss and a great chain in his hand. 2 And he mastered the dragon, the ancient serpent, who is the Devil and Satan, and bound him for a thousand years, 3 and cast him into the abyss and shut and sealed it upon him, that he might not any more deceive the nations, till the thousand years have been completed. Thereafter he must be let loose a little time. 4 Then I saw thrones, and they sat on them and judgment was given to them[1]—the souls of those beheaded for the witness of Jesus and the word of God, and whosoever had not worshipped the beast nor his image and had not received the mark on their foreheads and on their hands. They lived and reigned with Christ a thousand years. 5 The rest of the dead did not live until the thousand years were ended. 6 Blessed and holy is he who has part in this first resurrection. Over them the second death has not power, but they shall be priests of God and of Christ, and shall reign with Him the thousand years. 7 But when the thousand years are ended, Satan shall be loosed from his prison, 8 and shall come forth to deceive the nations which are in the four corners of the earth, Gog and Magog, to gather them to battle, their number being as the sand of the sea[2]. 9 They came up over the breadth of the earth and encircled the encampment of the saints, even the beloved city. But fire came down from heaven and consumed them[3]. 10 And the Devil who deceived them was cast into the lake of fire and brimstone, where are both the beast and the false prophet.

[1] Dan. vii. 22. And judgment was given to the saints of the Most High. [2] Ez. xxxviii. 2. Son of Man set thy face toward Gog of the land of Magog. *vv.* 15, 16. And thou shalt come from thy place out of the uttermost parts of the north, thou and many peoples with thee, all of them riding upon horses, a great company and a mighty army: and thou shalt come up against my people Israel, as a cloud to cover the land. [3] Ez. xxxviii. 22. And I will rain upon him and upon his hordes...great hailstones, fire and brimstone.

§ XXVIII

Ch. xx. 11—xxi. 1, 3–8, xxii. 18, 19, 21

11 Καὶ εἶδον θρόνον μέγαν λευκὸν καὶ τὸν καθήμενον ἐπ' αὐτόν, οὗ ἀπὸ τοῦ προσώπου ἔφυγεν ἡ γῆ καὶ ὁ οὐρανός, καὶ τόπος οὐχ εὑρέθη αὐτοῖς. 12 καὶ εἶδον τοὺς νεκροὺς τοὺς μεγάλους καὶ τοὺς μικροὺς ἑστῶτας ἐνώπιον τοῦ θρόνου, καὶ βιβλία ἠνοίχθησαν· καὶ ἄλλο βιβλίον ἠνοίχθη, ὅ ἐστιν τῆς ζωῆς· καὶ ἐκρίθησαν οἱ νεκροὶ ἐκ τῶν γεγραμμένων ἐν τοῖς βιβλίοις κατὰ τὰ ἔργα αὐτῶν. 13 καὶ ἔδωκεν ἡ θάλασσα τοὺς νεκροὺς τοὺς ἐπ' αὐτήν[1], καὶ ὁ θάνατος καὶ ὁ ᾅδης ἔδωκαν τοὺς νεκροὺς τοὺς ἐν αὐτοῖς, καὶ ἐκρίθησαν ἕκαστος κατὰ τὰ ἔργα αὐτῶν. 14 καὶ ὁ θάνατος καὶ ὁ ᾅδης ἐβλήθησαν εἰς τὴν λίμνην τοῦ πυρός. οὗτος ὁ θάνατος ὁ δεύτερός ἐστιν, * 15 καὶ εἴ τις οὐχ εὑρέθη ἐν τῇ βίβλῳ τῆς ζωῆς γεγραμμένος, ἐβλήθη εἰς τὴν λίμνην τοῦ πυρός. 1 Καὶ εἶδον οὐρανὸν καινὸν καὶ γῆν καινήν· ὁ γὰρ πρῶτος οὐρανὸς καὶ ἡ πρώτη γῆ ἀπῆλθαν, καὶ ἡ θάλασσα οὐκ ἔστιν ἔτι. * 3 καὶ ἤκουσα φωνῆς μεγάλης ἐκ τοῦ θρόνου λεγούσης· ἰδοὺ ἡ σκηνὴ τοῦ θεοῦ μετὰ τῶν ἀνθρώπων, καὶ σκηνώσει μετ' αὐτῶν, καὶ αὐτοὶ λαοὶ αὐτοῦ ἔσονται, καὶ αὐτὸς ὁ θεὸς ἔσται μετ' αὐτῶν, 4 * καὶ θάνατος οὐκ ἔσται ἔτι, οὔτε πένθος οὔτε κραυγὴ οὔτε πόνος οὐκ ἔσται ἔτι· ὅτι τὰ πρῶτα ἀπῆλθαν. 5 καὶ εἶπεν ὁ καθήμενος ἐπὶ τῷ θρόνῳ· ἰδοὺ καινὰ ποιῶ πάντα. * 6 ἐγὼ τὸ ἄλφα καὶ τὸ ω, ἡ ἀρχὴ καὶ τὸ τέλος. ἐγὼ τῷ διψῶντι δώσω αὐτῷ ἐκ τῆς πηγῆς τοῦ ὕδατος τῆς ζωῆς καὶ ὁ διψῶν ἐρχέσθω, ὁ θέλων λαβέτω δωρεάν. 7 ὁ νικῶν κληρονομήσει ταῦτα, καὶ ἔσομαι αὐτῷ θεὸς καὶ αὐτὸς ἔσται μοι υἱός. 8 τοῖς δὲ δειλοῖς καὶ ἀπίστοις καὶ ἐβδελυγμένοις καὶ φονεῦσιν καὶ πόρνοις καὶ φαρμακοῖς καὶ εἰδωλολάτραις καὶ πᾶσιν τοῖς ψευδέσιν τὸ μέρος αὐτῶν ἐν τῇ λίμνῃ τῇ καιομένῃ πυρὶ καὶ θείῳ, ὅ ἐστιν ὁ θάνατος ὁ δεύτερος. 18 Μαρτυρῶ ἐγὼ παντὶ τῷ ἀκούοντι τοὺς λόγους τῆς προφητείας τοῦ βιβλίου τούτου· ἐάν τις ἐπιθῇ ἐπ' αὐτά, ἐπιθήσει ἐπ' αὐτὸν ὁ θεὸς τὰς πληγὰς τὰς γεγραμμένας ἐν τῷ βιβλίῳ τούτῳ· 19 καὶ ἐάν τις ἀφέλῃ ἀπὸ τῶν λόγων τοῦ βιβλίου τῆς προφητείας ταύτης, ἀφελεῖ ὁ θεὸς τὸ μέρος αὐτοῦ ἀπὸ τοῦ ξύλου τῆς ζωῆς καὶ ἐκ τῆς πόλεως τῆς ἁγίας. 21 Ἡ χάρις τοῦ κυρίου Ἰησοῦ μετὰ πάντων.

[1] Geb. ἐν αὐτῇ.

§ XXVIII

The Final State

xx. 11 Then I saw a great white throne and Him who sat on it, from whose face the earth and the heavens had fled, and place was not found for them. 12 I saw the dead, great and small, standing before the throne and rolls were opened[1]. Also another roll was opened, that of life. From what was written in the rolls the dead were judged according to their works. 13 The sea gave up the dead that were by it, and death and Hades gave up the dead that were in them, and each was judged according to his works. 14 Then death and Hades were cast into the lake of fire[2]. This is the second death 15 that if anyone was not found written in the roll of life, he was cast into the lake of fire[3]. xxi. 1 Then I saw a new kind of heaven and a new kind of earth; for the former heaven and the former earth have passed away, and the sea is not any more. 3 And I heard a great voice from the throne saying: Lo the dwelling-place of God is with men, and He will dwell with them and they themselves shall be His people and God Himself shall be with them. 4 Death shall be no more[2]. Nor shall grief, nor wailing, nor distress be any more[4], for the former things have passed away. 5 He who sat on the throne said: Lo I make all things new. 6 I am the alpha and the omega, the beginning and the end. I will give to him that thirsts of the fountain of the water of life and whosoever thirsts, let him come, and whosoever will, let him take freely. 7 He who overcomes shall inherit these things; and I shall be to him God, and he will be to me a son. 8 But to the fearing and unbelieving, and those taking part in abominations, and murderers and fornicators and sorcerers and those who serve idols, and all liars, their portion is in the lake which burns with fire and brimstone, which is the second death. xxii. 18 I witness to all who hear the words of the prophecy of this book: if anyone add to them, God will add to him the plagues written in this book; 19 and if anyone take away from the words of the book of this prophecy, God will take away his part from the tree of life and from the holy city. 21 The grace of the Lord Jesus be with all.

[1] Dan. vii. 9. I beheld till thrones were placed and one that was ancient of days did sit...the judgment was set and the books were opened. [2] Is. xxv. 8. He hath swallowed up death for ever and the Lord God shall wipe away tears from off all faces. [3] Is. lxix. 28. Let them be blotted out of the book of life, and not be written with the righteous. [4] Is. xxxv. 10. And everlasting joy shall be upon their heads: they shall obtain gladness and joy, and sorrow and sighing shall flee away.

Doublets

References to the original in brackets

Editor's Introduction

i. 1 Ἀποκάλυψις Ἰησοῦ Χριστοῦ, ἣν ἔδωκεν αὐτῷ ὁ θεός, δεῖξαι τοῖς δούλοις αὐτοῦ ἃ δεῖ γενέσθαι ἐν τάχει, καὶ ἐσήμανεν ἀποστείλας διὰ τοῦ ἀγγέλου αὐτοῦ τῷ δούλῳ αὐτοῦ Ἰωάννῃ, 2 ὃς ἐμαρτύρησεν τὸν λόγον τοῦ θεοῦ καὶ τὴν μαρτυρίαν Ἰησοῦ Χριστοῦ, ὅσα ἴδεν. (xxii. 6–8, i. 9.) 4 Ἰωάννης ταῖς ἑπτὰ ἐκκλησίαις ταῖς ἐν τῇ Ἀσίᾳ· (i. 11.) ἀπὸ ὁ ὢν καὶ ὁ ἦν καὶ ὁ ἐρχόμενος, (iv. 8.) καὶ ἀπὸ τῶν ἑπτὰ πνευμάτων ἃ ἐνώπιον τοῦ θρόνου αὐτοῦ. (iv. 5.) 7 ναί ἀμήν. (xxii. 20.) 8 ἐγώ εἰμι τὸ ἄλφα καὶ τὸ ω, λέγει κύριος ὁ θεός, ὁ ὢν καὶ ὁ ἦν καὶ ὁ ἐρχόμενος, ὁ παντοκράτωρ. (xxi. 6, iv. 8.)

§ II. ii. 7, 11 and 17 and § III. ii. 29 and iii. 6 and § IV. III. 13: ὁ ἔχων οὖς ἀκουσάτω τί τὸ πνεῦμα λέγει ταῖς ἐκκλησίαις. (iii. 22.)

§ VI. xi. 7 τὸ ἀναβαῖνον ἐκ τῆς ἀβύσσου. (xvii. 8.)

§ IX. xiii. 9 εἴ τις ἔχει οὖς, ἀκουσάτω. (iii. 22.)

§ XI. viii. 7 Καὶ ὁ πρῶτος ἐσάλπισεν· καὶ ἐβλήθη εἰς τὴν γῆν· καὶ τὸ τρίτον τῆς γῆς κατεκάη, κατεκάη. 8 Καὶ ὁ δεύτερος ἄγγελος ἐσάλπισεν· ἐβλήθη εἰς τὴν θάλασσαν· καὶ ἐγένετο τὸ τρίτον τῆς θαλάσσης αἷμα, 9 καὶ ἀπέθανεν τὸ τρίτον τῶν κτισμάτων τῶν ἐν τῇ θαλάσσῃ, τὰ ἔχοντα ψυχάς, καὶ τὸ τρίτον τῶν πλοίων διεφθάρησαν. 10 Καὶ ὁ τρίτος ἄγγελος ἐσάλπισεν· 12 Καὶ ὁ τέταρτος ἄγγελος ἐσάλπισεν· καὶ ἐπλήγη τὸ τρίτον τοῦ ἡλίου καὶ τὸ τρίτον τῆς σελήνης καὶ τὸ τρίτον τῶν ἀστέρων, ἵνα σκοτισθῇ τὸ τρίτον αὐτῶν καὶ ἡ ἡμέρα μὴ φάνῃ τὸ τρίτον αὐτῆς, καὶ ἡ νὺξ ὁμοίως. (xvi. 2–4, viii. 5, 6, ix. 2, vi. 12.) xvi. 2 τοὺς ἔχοντας τὸ χάραγμα τοῦ θηρίου καὶ τοὺς προσκυνοῦντας τῇ εἰκόνι αὐτοῦ. (xiii. 10, 17.) 3 αἷμα. (*v.* 4.) 9 τοῦ ἔχοντος τὴν ἐξουσίαν (xi. 6.) 12 τὸν μέγαν. (ix. 14.)

§ XIII. xvi. 19 ἡ μεγάλη. (*v.* 19.) 21 καὶ ἐβλασφήμησαν οἱ ἄνθρωποι τὸν θεὸν ἐκ τῆς πληγῆς τῆς χαλάζης. (xvi. 9 and 11.)

§ XIV. xvii. 11 καὶ εἰς ἀπώλειαν ὑπάγει. (*v.* 8.)

§ XV. xviii. 10 ἡ πόλις ἡ μεγάλη. (*v.* 15.) 15 ἀπὸ μακρόθεν στήσονται διὰ τὸν φόβον τοῦ βασανισμοῦ αὐτῆς. 17 ἀπὸ μακρόθεν. 18 βλέποντες τὸν καπνὸν τῆς πυρώσεως αὐτῆς. (*vv.* 9–10.)

Doublets

Editor's Introduction

i. 1 An apocalypse of Jesus Christ, which God gave him to show to His servants what must come to pass shortly. And he signified, having sent by His angel to His servant John 2 who witnessed the word of God and the witness of Jesus Christ, those things he saw. 4 John to the seven churches which are in Asia. From the one who is, who was and is to come, and from the seven spirits that are before His throne. 7 Yea, Amen. 8 I am the alpha and the omega, says the Lord God, the one who is, who was and who is to come, the All-sovereign.

§ II. ii. 7, 11 and 17 and § III. ii. 29 and iii. 6 and § IV. iii. 13: He who has an ear, let him hear what the Spirit says to the churches.

§ VI. xi. 7 that comes up from the abyss.

§ IX. xiii. 9 If any one has an ear, let him hear.

§ XI. viii. 7–12 And the first sounded...and it was cast on the earth. And the third of the earth was burned,...was burned. And the second angel sounded...was cast into the sea: and the third of the sea became blood, and the third of the creatures that were in the sea, those having life, died, and the third of the ships were destroyed. And the third angel sounded. And the fourth angel sounded. And a third of the sun was smitten and a third of the moon and a third of the stars, in order that the third of them should be darkened, and the day, the third of it, might not show, and the night similarly. xvi. 2 those who have the mark of the beast and those worshipping his image. 3 blood...him who has power. 12 the great.

§ XIII. xvi. 19 great. 21 And men blasphemed God because of the plague of the hail.

§ XIV. xvii. 11 and it subjects to destruction.

§ XV. xviii. 10 the Great City. 15 shall stand far away from fear of her trial. 17 afar off. 18 seeing the smoke of her burning.

§ XVI. xix. 5 οἱ μικροὶ καὶ οἱ μεγάλοι. (xiii. 16.)

§ XVII. v. 5 καὶ φωναὶ καὶ βρονταί. (xvi. 18.) 9 τῷ καθημένῳ ἐπὶ τῷ θρόνῳ τῷ ζῶντι εἰς τοὺς αἰῶνας τῶν αἰώνων. (v. 10.)

§ XIX. vi. 3 καὶ ὅτε ἤνοιξεν τὴν σφραγῖδα τὴν δευτέραν, ἤκουσα τοῦ δευτέρου ζώου λέγοντος· ἔρχου. 5 καὶ ὅτε ἤνοιξεν τὴν σφραγῖδα τὴν τρίτην, ἤκουσα τοῦ τρίτου ζώου λέγοντος· ἔρχου. 7 καὶ ὅτε ἤνοιξεν τὴν σφραγῖδα τὴν τετάρτην, ἤκουσα φωνὴν τοῦ τετάρτου ζώου λέγοντος· ἔρχου. 9 ὅτε ἤνοιξεν τὴν πέμπτην σφραγῖδα. 12 καὶ ὅτε ἤνοιξεν τὴν σφραγῖδα τὴν ἕκτην. (v. 1.)

§ XX. vii. 2 οἷς ἐδόθη αὐτοῖς ἀδικῆσαι τὴν γῆν καὶ τὴν θάλασσαν. (v. 3.) 5 ἐκ φυλῆς Ἰούδα δώδεκα χιλιάδες ἐσφραγισμένοι, ἐκ φυλῆς Ῥουβὴν δώδεκα χιλιάδες, ἐκ φυλῆς Γὰδ δώδεκα χιλιάδες, 6 ἐκ φυλῆς Ἀσὴρ δώδεκα χιλιάδες, ἐκ φυλῆς Νεφθαλεὶμ δώδεκα χιλιάδες, ἐκ φυλῆς Μανασσῆ δώδεκα χιλιάδες, 7 ἐκ φυλῆς Συμεὼν δώδεκα χιλιάδες, ἐκ φυλῆς Λευεὶ δώδεκα χιλιάδες, ἐκ φυλῆς Ἰσσάχαρ δώδεκα χιλιάδες, 8 ἐκ φυλῆς Ζαβουλὼν δώδεκα χιλιάδες, ἐκ φυλῆς Ἰωσὴφ δώδεκα χιλιάδες, ἐκ φυλῆς Βενιαμεὶν δώδεκα χιλιάδες ἐσφραγισμένοι. (v. 4.)

§ XXI. viii. 5 καὶ ἐγένοντο βρονταὶ καὶ φωναὶ καὶ ἀστραπαὶ καὶ σεισμός. (xvi. 18.) 6 ἑπτά. xvi. 6 ἄξιοί εἰσιν. (iii. 4.) viii. 13 τριῶν. λοιπῶν. ix. 2 ἐκ τοῦ καπνοῦ τοῦ φρέατος. (v. 2.) 4 τὸν χόρτον τῆς γῆς οὐδὲ πᾶν χλωρὸν οὐδὲ πᾶν δένδρον. (viii. 7.)

§ XXII. ix. 18 ἀπὸ τῶν τριῶν πληγῶν τούτων ἀπεκτάνθησαν τὸ τρίτον τῶν ἀνθρώπων, ἐκ τοῦ πυρὸς καὶ τοῦ καπνοῦ καὶ τοῦ θείου τοῦ ἐκπορευομένου ἐκ τῶν στομάτων αὐτῶν. (v. 15, v. 17.)

§ XXIII. xi. 18 τοῖς μικροῖς καὶ τοῖς μεγάλοις. (xiii. 16.) 19 καὶ ἐγένοντο ἀστραπαὶ καὶ φωναὶ καὶ βρονταὶ καὶ σεισμὸς καὶ χάλαζα μεγάλη. (xvi. 18 and 21.) xiv. 8 Καὶ ἄλλος ἄγγελος δεύτερος ἠκολούθησεν λέγων· ἔπεσεν ἔπεσεν Βαβυλὼν ἡ μεγάλη, ἣ ἐκ τοῦ οἴνου τοῦ θυμοῦ τῆς πορνείας αὐτῆς πεπότικεν πάντα τὰ ἔθνη. (xviii. 1–3.) 11 καὶ ὁ καπνὸς τοῦ βασανισμοῦ αὐτῶν εἰς αἰῶνας αἰώνων ἀναβαίνει, (v. 10, xix. 3.) καὶ οὐκ ἔχουσιν ἀνάπαυσιν ἡμέρας καὶ νύκτας (iv. 8) οἱ προσκυνοῦντες τὸ θηρίον καὶ τὴν εἰκόνα αὐτοῦ, καὶ εἴ τις λαμβάνει τὸ χάραγμα τοῦ ὀνόματος αὐτοῦ. (xiv. 9.)

§ XXV. xxi. 19 ὁ θεμέλιος ὁ πρῶτος. ὁ δεύτερος. ὁ τρίτος. ὁ τέταρτος. 20 ὁ πέμπτος. ὁ ἕκτος. ὁ ἕβδομος. ὁ ὄγδοος. ὁ ἔνατος. ὁ δέκατος. ὁ ἑνδέκατος. ὁ δωδέκατος. (v. 14.)

§ XVI. xix. 5 small and great.

§ XVII. v. 5 and voices and thunders. 9 to Him who sits on the throne—the living one to ages of ages.

§ XIX. vi. 3 And when he had opened the second seal, I heard the second living creature saying, Come. 5 And when he had opened the third seal, I heard the third living creature saying, Come. 7 And when he had opened the fourth seal, I heard the voice of the fourth living creature say, Come. 9 When he had opened the fifth seal. 12 And when he had opened the sixth seal.

§ XX. vii. 2 to whom it was given to hurt the land and the sea. 5–8 Of the tribe of Judah were sealed twelve thousand, of the tribe of Reuben twelve thousand, of the tribe of Gad twelve thousand, of the tribe of Asher twelve thousand, of the tribe of Naphtali twelve thousand, of the tribe of Manasseh twelve thousand, of the tribe of Simeon twelve thousand, of the tribe of Levi twelve thousand, of the tribe of Issachar twelve thousand, of the tribe of Zebulon twelve thousand, of the tribe of Joseph twelve thousand, of the tribe of Benjamin twelve thousand were sealed.

§ XXI. viii. 5 Then were there thunders, voices and lightnings, and earthquake. 6 seven. xvi. 6 Worthy are they! viii. 13 three...rest. ix. 2 from the smoke of the pit. 4 the pasture of the earth, nor aught green, nor any tree.

§ XXII. ix. 18 By these three plagues were killed the third of mankind, even from the fire, the smoke, the brimstone which go forth from their mouths.

§ XXIII. xi. 18 to small and to great. 19 and there were lightnings and voices, thunders and earthquake and great hail. xiv. 8 And another, a second angel, followed, saying: Fallen, fallen is Babylon the Great! which from the wine of her fornication intoxicated all nations. 11 and the smoke of their testing goes up for ages of ages. Nor have they rest day and night who worship the beast and his image, yea, if anyone receive the mark of his name.

§ XXV. xxi. 19 the first foundation. the second. the third. the fourth. 20 the fifth. the sixth. the seventh. the eighth. the ninth. the tenth. the eleventh. the twelfth.

§ XXVI. xxi. 24 *φέρουσιν τὴν δόξαν αὐτῶν εἰς αὐτήν.* (*v.* 26.) 27 *εἰ μὴ οἱ γεγραμμένοι ἐν τῷ βιβλίῳ τῆς ζωῆς τοῦ ἀρνίου.* (xiii. 8.) xxii. 1 *καὶ τοῦ ἀρνίου.* (*v.* 3.) 3 *τοῦ θεοῦ καὶ.* (*v.* 1.) 5 *καὶ νὺξ οὐκ ἔσται ἔτι,* (xxi. 25.) *καὶ βασιλεύσουσιν εἰς τοὺς αἰῶνας τῶν αἰώνων.* (xi. 15.) 13 *ἐγὼ τὸ ἄλφα καὶ τὸ ω, ὁ πρῶτος καὶ ὁ ἔσχατος, ἡ ἀρχὴ καὶ τὸ τέλος.* (xxi. 6.) 7 *καὶ ἰδοὺ ἔρχομαι ταχύ.* (*v.* 12.) *μακάριος ὁ τηρῶν τοὺς λόγους τῆς προφητείας τοῦ βιβλίου τούτου.* (*v.* 10 and i. 3.) 9 *καὶ τῶν τηρούντων τοὺς λόγους τοῦ βιβλίου τούτου.* (*v.* 7.) xix. 9, 10 *καὶ λέγει μοι· οὗτοι οἱ λόγοι ἀληθινοὶ τοῦ θεοῦ ἐστίν. καὶ ἔπεσα ἔμπροσθεν τῶν ποδῶν αὐτοῦ προσκυνῆσαι αὐτῷ. καὶ λέγει μοι· ὅρα μή. σύνδουλός σου εἰμὶ καὶ τῶν ἀδελφῶν σου. τῷ θεῷ προσκύνησον.* (xxii. 6, 8, 9.) xxii. 17 *ὕδωρ ζωῆς δωρέαν* (xxi. 6.) 20 *ἔρχομαι ταχύ* (*v.* 12.)

§ XXVII. xx. 5 *αὕτη ἡ ἀνάστασις ἡ πρώτη.* (*v.* 6). 10 *καὶ βασανισθήσονται ἡμέρας καὶ νυκτὸς εἰς τοὺς αἰῶνας τῶν αἰώνων.* (xiv. 11.)

§ XXVIII. xx. 14 *ἡ λίμνη τοῦ πυρός.* (*v.* 14.) xxi. 2 *καὶ τὴν πόλιν τὴν ἁγίαν Ἱερουσαλὴμ καινὴν εἶδον καταβαίνουσαν ἐκ τοῦ οὐρανοῦ ἀπὸ τοῦ θεοῦ.* (xxi. 10.) 4 *καὶ ἐξαλείψει πᾶν δάκρυον ἐκ τῶν ὀφθαλμῶν αὐτῶν.* (vii. 17.) 5 *καὶ λέγει· γράψον, ὅτι οὗτοι οἱ λόγοι πιστοὶ καὶ ἀληθινοί εἰσιν.* (xix. 9.) 6 *καὶ εἶπέν μοι· γέγοναν.* (xvi. 17.)

§ XXVI. xxi. 24 into her they bring their glory. 27 none save those written in the Lamb's book of life. xxii. 1 and of the Lamb. 3 of God and. 5 And there shall be no night there, and they shall reign for ever and ever. 13 I am the alpha and the omega, the first and the last, the beginning and the end. xxii. 7 And behold I come soon. Blessed is he who keeps the sayings of the prophecy of this book. 9 and of those keeping the words of this book. xix. 9, 10 And he says to me, These are the true words of God. And I fell down to worship at his feet. But he says to me: See thou do it not. I am a fellow-servant of thee and of thy brethren. Worship God. 17 The water of life freely. 20 I come quickly.

§ XXVII. xx. 5 This is the first resurrection. 10 They shall be tormented day and night for ever and ever.

§ XXVIII. xx. 14 the lake of fire. xxi. 2 Then I saw the city, the new holy Jerusalem, coming down out of heaven from God. 4 And he shall wipe away every tear from their eyes. 5 And He says: Write that these are the faithful and true words. 6 Then He said to me: They have come to pass.

SOME POINTS OF CRITICISM

AN adequate discussion of the above order would require a full and consecutive exposition, upon which I do not propose to enter. But some criticisms have been offered, to which answers may be helpful.

The first concerns the whole view of the book. The view, which has been most widely accepted, is that it is a collection from many sources of excerpts crudely put together. As the gaps and confusion are the facts upon which this conclusion rests, any attempt to remove them is regarded as erring from the start.

On such matters there is always room for difference of judgment, but, for myself, the more I have studied the book the more incredible this theory has become. There may have been other persons who wrote Greek in this peculiar Hebrew idiom, but is it likely that there were many who wrote it with the same power? Among them, is it likely that there were many who knew the O.T. with the fullness and ease which could allow it to be so perfectly woven into the writer's own style and presentation? Above all there is the gift for doing it with an eloquence and picturesqueness which never flags. Where the work is continuous, the sequence, though not logical in form, is always close and usually clear: and the whole seems to present one singularly individual Apocalyptic outlook. In short, what John Sterling said of Carlyle's letter can be said of Revelation, that the author has not signed it merely in one place, but in every line. Nor does it seem to me credible that anyone who could so mould the O.T. to his purpose, should fail entirely to mould into one anything else he may have borrowed.

Some other explanation, therefore, would seem to be needed, the test of which ought to be the production of a closer connexion and a clearer sequence. As a general principle, indeed, there could be no other object in criticising any text, or any evidence of success, except as this is accomplished. But instead of Revelation being the kind of book we are not even to try to make more connected, it seems to me in a very high degree the kind of mixture of clearness and confusion which challenges us to make the attempt.

Mostly this has been done by assuming very extensive alterations of text of a somewhat deliberate kind. For two reasons this seems to me improbable. First, redactions would surely be intended to smoothe away difficulties, and not to create them. Secondly, would an ancient scribe have undertaken such a task in face of the terrible curse against adding to or taking from its words, with which the book closes? As a matter of fact, the text has probably come down to us from the first editor in a quite exceptional state of purity, as we should expect with such a document. That the theory here offered assumes throughout a meticulous, if not always intelligent care, not to omit any word, or, beyond repetition, to add, does surely add to its probability.

The change which is most decisive for the new order suggested is the position, at the beginning of the new prophecy after the Messages to the Churches, assigned to ch. x (p. 52), because, if this is granted, the rest follows almost inevitably.

For this change some reasons have been given (p. 8), but two objections have been raised which were not discussed. The one concerns "another angel" in *v.* 1 and the other "the days of the seventh angel" in *v.* 7. In the new connexion, it is objected there is no first angel and the seventh angel has not been introduced.

Where the passage now stands, both references present difficulties. Before it, we have the sixth angel. Then we have four more: and these turn out to be hosts. Afterwards we have to do with men and not angels. Elsewhere, even when there are only two more, "another angel" is further distinguished as a third. Again, where the passage now stands, the reference to the seventh angel certainly comes after the sixth and before the seventh, but difficulty arises the moment we try to realise the situation.

John is in the midst of a great vision of woes. After ix. 21, this continues at xi. 14 as though it had not been interrupted. Apparently it is unfolded from a great roll in heaven, and seen from the standpoint of heaven. But now John is on Patmos, and an angel comes to him with a little roll of prophecy, which goes into matters quite irrelevant to the vision of the woes. The seven thunders, which are nowhere introduced, reveal mysteries, which are to be sealed up till the days of the seventh angel. But what end would that serve, if we have already arrived in the narrative at those days? Moreover, when the angel swears that there is to be no more delay, or that the allotted time is nearly spent, the assurance is far more likely to be addressed to John's own contemporaries, and not to be a mere dramatic incident in a vision of remote events. It is still far enough away to make it necessary for the seer to prophesy again, like the ancient prophets, so that it appears to be only another form of "Lo I come quickly" which is the presupposition of the whole book. In fact the whole passage from x. 1 to xi. 13 is a quite impossible interruption.

In the new position, we only need to remember that all John's visions are shown him by angels, to see who the first angel is. In the Messages, which immediately precede in this order, the angel is only a voice speaking behind him, plainly from heaven. But John is with this angel in Patmos: and the rest is only vision. That the angel remains present appears from his speaking in x. 8: and that it is the same angel as showed the first vision is seen from the instructions he gives about the new prophecy, which are much the same as about the last. A new angel joining him, therefore, is another angel.

The "days of the seventh angel" seems to be another example of the many summaries in the book, which sum up rapidly what only the detailed narrative which follows fully explains. The fulfilment seems to be in xv. 1 (p. 88) and that this is now in the days of the seventh angel, is another point in favour of the new order. Thus instead of assuming that we have already come to the days of the seventh angel, we have only entered on the narrative which will end with it: and, therefore, we are to assume that they are as far apart as the narrative will allow. In that case, the editor's arrangement would merely be another of several cases of making connexions by words, without much regard to the sense.

The transposition of shorter passages from one section to

another raises another kind of question. But the transference only of xv. 6–8 (p. 12) has so far been criticised. The passage was said to read quite well in its present context, and even to be necessary for introducing the angels with the seven woes.

The difficulties at this point are perhaps the greatest in the book, and there may well be some better solution of them than mine. Yet for this particular case, I think, a fairly good justification can be offered. First, the angels of the plagues and the angels of the last plagues are different, because, among other reasons, one of the angels of the plagues introduces John to the Great City, Babylon, and one of the angels of the last plagues introduces him to the Holy City, Jerusalem. A weighty argument for the new order is that it shows the reason to be that the first set of angels prepare for judgment on Babylon, and the second for the introduction of the Holy Jerusalem. But one section (§ XI) is too long and the other (§ XXIV) is too short by the exact length of this description. Therefore, the transference is a very obvious conclusion, especially, as has already been explained (p. 12), the editor would need to make it, if he wrongly identified the angels. When the passage is restored, as in § XXIV, the angels of the last plagues complete their work, and the song of rejoicing naturally follows: whereas, isolated as xv. 1 is, they are left doing nothing. On the other hand, in the new connexion in § XI, the angels which fulfil prophecy naturally come out of the ark of testimony and need no introduction.

The very remarkable accuracy with which the longer restorations work out on the rigid standards of length and glosses, seem to me to guarantee them with fair certainty. There, is, however, no such security about the shorter emendations. For example, in § XXIV, I am not at all sure that xv. 6c, "girt about the breasts etc" is not a doublet merely with the politer word breasts for paps and that "small and great" in xi. 19 in the previous section, which goes with it, should not stand instead. Of the rest I have most uncertainty about § XXVI. There seem to be transferences from it and to it of a kind not found in any other section: and, if this is right, it suggests that being the editor's last page, there was some problem of making its length exact.

One other change I made after the book was in proof. xiv. 1–5 and 6–12 were transposed. Only then did I observe that the latter passage, as it stood after the omission of doublets, was almost exactly the same length as the former. This transposition transfers them from and to § X and § XXIII, and there the length fits the sections exactly.

xiv. 6–12, where it now is in § X, follows perfectly the account of the worship of the beast. xiv. 1–5, where it stands in the text, is a pure interruption, and without any preparation in what goes before, or any connexion with what follows. Where it now stands in § XXIII, the Messiah and the hundred and forty and four thousand saints, who return with him to establish God's kingdom in the earth, naturally appear in triumph and praise in Mount Zion, after their victory. And after this, it is equally natural to give an account of the departed saints who do not return, before passing on to the descent of the new order from heaven.

§ XII might seem to introduce the heavenly powers too soon. But only in the previous section is a battle set and the beast and the false prophet mentioned together. Besides, in the fall of all the monarchies, the invisible powers which fulfil God's word are concerned, and, naturally, this is more dramatically staged with the fall of Rome. The visible forces would still be the Eastern armies.

Printed in the United States
By Bookmasters